# The Making of a Hero

## Apostle Elizabeth Itegi

*Foreword by* **Dr. Gwyneth & Pst Star Williams**
*Edited by*: **Rev Tony Kimani, M.Div.**

Copyright © 2016 by Elizabeth Itegi

Printed in the United States of America

First Printing, 2016

ISBN-13: 978-1537304960

ISBN-10: 1537304968

**Published by:**
**Tony Kimani Press, Inc.**
**1084 Woodland Ave SE**
**Atlanta, GA 30316**
**Cell# (404) 552-1036**

# Dedication

To my husband and our four Children:
Evelyn, Edwin, Grace, & Yvonne. My
son in law, Tony and all my
grandchildren.

# Foreword

Apostle Elizabeth Itegi is a powerful and anointed woman of God. She knows and cherishes the power of God and her heart is for the nations. She has been ordained as an Apostle to the nations and is passionate about her call.

The book, *The Making of a Hero,* is a reflection of who she is and the destiny she is pursuing. The author has been destined for greatness since she was a child. Her perseverance, tenacity, prayer life are the fruits of her undying faith and are evident. She has been sent to America by God's hand and His divine providence.

When you read this book it will change your life for eternity. You will be inspired to take a leap of faith to do what seems impossible, but by her testimony you will have a living example. She is a game changer, walking out her destiny and purpose from nothing to something.

"Most assuredly, I say to you, he who believes in Me, the works that I do he will do also; and greater works than these he will do, because I go to My Father." John 14:12

Blessings & Empowerment,
Dr. Gwyneth & Pastor Star Williams
lifeenrichmentinc.com

# Table of Contents

# 1

# Humble

# Beginnings

# Humble Beginnings

*"Do not despise these small beginnings, for the Lord rejoices to see the work begin, to see the plumb line in Zerubbabel's hand."*

## Zec. 4:10 (NLT)

To God our Father, be Glory now and forever more. I bless His holy name.

I am so humbled to write this book to exalt my maker and to let people know how great God is. God is wonderful and through Him I am standing today and I can write about His mercies and goodness, which endures from generations to generations.

I was born in Kenya - a blessed nation in East Africa whose 80% of population are Christians. I come from a very humble back ground, but by the Grace of God our Father I can stand and testify of His faithfulness. God has been faithful to me and my family; I have seen Him take me from one Glory to another. In June 13th, 2006 I moved from Kenya to the United States of America when God spoke to me through *Genesis 12: 1*

*'Go out of your country, from your family and from your father's house, to a land that I will show you. I will make you a great Nation I will bless you and make your name great and you shall be a blessing. I will bless those who bless you, and I will curse those who curse you. And in you all the families of the earth shall be blessed.'*

When I learned that God's will is for me to move out of my own country and culture, I started praying and looking for my path to my destiny. God convinced me that He wanted me to go to the United States of America. In the year 2005, God put a desire of praying for the U.S.A and I started loving it. Any information pertaining United States of America could tickle my heart and I'd give it attention unreservedly. Every single day I prayed for U.S.A and I possessed it. Some people were so offended at my conviction and confession that U.S.A is my land. However, I didn't change my desire until God opened a door for me to come to the United States of America where I have been since June 2006.

Before we landed to London's Heathrow
Airport, the Lord spoke to me and told
me: *wake up and open your bible* in
*Isaiah 45:2-4*

> *'I will go before you and make the
> crooked places straight I will
> break in pieces the gates of
> bronze, and cut the bars of iron. I
> will give you treasures of darkness
> and hidden riches of secret
> places. That you may know
> that I, the Lord who call you by
> your name. I am the God of Israel.'*

I woke up and read that entire message;
merged it with the first message and
gained more confidence in the lord. On
landing in the United States of America
things were not so smooth. My hosts
started talking negative: how things are
very tough in U.S.A, it was not the right
time for me to come; I should go back to
Kenya and wait until when things will be
okay. I chose not to give attention to
every negative voice and word because I
knew very well it was my best time to
relocate to the U.S.A. I was not so sure
of my next move, but I decided to fast
and pray. God gave me this word in the

book of *Jeremiah 17:5-8*

> *'Cursed is the man who trust in man, and make flesh his strength. Blessed is the man who trust I the Lord and whose hope is the Lord, for he shall be like a tree planted by the waters which spreads out its roots by the river, and will not fear when heat comes but its leaf will be green and will not be anxious in the year of drought, nor cease from yielding fruit.'*

I experienced difficulties in the process of settling down and God's Grace has been sufficient all the time. When God called you and gave you a promise, you should know that the devil also appeared and heard what God said concerning your life. What the devil tries to do is *to steal, and to kill and to destroy (John 10:10).*

I realized that there is a war ahead of me. The devil tries to oppose us through fear and intimidation until we grow weary and lose hope and direction. I tell you today that it's not time to quit or lose hope. We should stand and pray and trust in God.

*Psalms 125:1 'Those who trust in the Lord are like mount Zion which cannot be moved, but abides forever*

# 2

# Trust
# in
# God

# Trust in God

*"Trust in the LORD with all your heart
and lean not on your own
understanding"*
*Prov. 3:5 (NIV)*

Those who love God and are called by
His name, should trust in God totally
*Proverbs 3:5- 6 'Trust in the Lord
with all your heart and lean not on
your own understanding in all
ways acknowledge Him and He
shall direct your paths.'*
When you totally trust in God in
everything you do and wherever you go,
you will never be shaken or moved.
*Daniel 11:32 'Those who know their God
shall be mighty and do exploits.'*
It's time to know that God is on your
side to give you total victory. Don't
allow the enemy to lie to you, telling
how powerless you are, how your people
didn't make and you are no exception.
Those who were before you had their
opportunity. You are chosen of God to
make a difference in your family and
community because you are God's

instrument of change.

> *1 Peter 2:9-10 'But you are a chosen generation, a royal priesthood, a holy nation, its own special people, that you may proclaim the praises of him who called you out of darkness into His marvelous light, who once were not a people but are now the people of God who had not obtained mercy but now you have obtained mercy.'*

Let people now know that God has entirely changed you and your all for his own honor and glory. Jesus Christ worked for you to make you a new creation; and works on you to make you a victor, a conqueror.

> *Isaiah 43:18-19 'Do not remember the former things, nor consider the thing of old. Behold I will do a new thing Now it shall spring forth, shall you not know it. I will even make a road in the wilderness, And rivers in the desert'*

I was the least in my family; with nothing, not even the best education. Today, I am greatly blessed for I know who I am

*I Corinthians 2:9 'Eye has not seen, nor ear heard nor have entered into the heart of man The things which God has prepared for those who Love Him.'*

The heavenly realm has all the blessings for you. Don't lose heart or feel left out. God is not done with us yet. He is continually working on us, molding and shaping us so that we can fit in His plans and purposes. God has chosen and called you to make a vessel of Honor. God has made you the Son He is so proud of. You are nothing less of His Son. God made you; created you in his likeness and image and so you are fearfully and wonderfully made. Don't be infuriated by men or the devil; you are the hero of God. God is counting on you.

# 3

# God's

# Hero

# God's Hero

*"Arise, shine for your light has come and the glory of the Lord is risen upon you".*
*Isaiah 60:1*

Do you know it's time for you to arise and shine now? You are called to arise and shine for Jesus. Nobody else in your family, school, working place, community or church will arise and shine except you. You are a Hero of Faith. A Hero is a persistent person and has the ability to pursue and get what belongs to him or her; a winner; a determined person.

When I was being brought up, there were no believers in our family though we used to go to church once in a while. We were not saved, until when I got married became a wife and a mother that Jesus revealed Himself to me, He spoke to me:

> *John 3:16-17 'For God so loved the world that He gave his only begotten son, that whoever*

*believes in Him should not perish but have everlasting life. For God didn't send His son into the world to condemn the world, but the world through Him might be saved.'*

These words hit me so hard that I could not divert my attention. The Holy Spirit convicted me. After a while I received Jesus Christ as my Lord and Savior. I know that I belong to God and my name is written in the Lamb book of life.

*Psalms 32: 1-2 'Blessed is he whose transgression is forgiven whose sin is covered. Blessed is the man to whom the Lord does not impute iniquity and in whose spirit there is No deceit.'*

God, through His son's completed work at the cross, has made me Holy and Righteous and I have become an heir in His kingdom.

*John 1:12 'Those who received Him He gave them power to become the sons of God who were not born of blood, nor of the will of flesh, nor of the will of man but God. '*

God has called you to be his vessel of

honor; the reason you were bought of a price. Jesus Christ shed His blood at the cross at Calvary for your freedom. He accomplished all and said *it is finished.*

*Romans 10:9- 10 'If thou shall confess with thy mouth, the Lord Jesus and shall believe in thy heart that God has raised Him from the dead thou shall be saved. For with the heart man believeth unto righteousness, and with the mouth confession is made unto salvation.'*

It's not about our good work or behavior but the accomplished work at the cross. Jesus left nothing behind to be done by a human being except to receive the savior and make him your Lord and follow Him all the days of your life. When God revealed to me what Jesus did for me I confessed it until I was transformed. Every word of God, every vision, every prophecy comes in your life so that it can focus you on the knowledge of the plans of God concerning your life. God doesn't call the qualified ones but he qualifies the ones he calls. When God calls you He makes sure that's you follow Him having nothing so that what He gives you is for His glory. Genesis 12:1

When he wanted to use Moses He appeared to him in the wilderness in a burning bush:

> *Exodus 3:2 'And the angel of the Lord appeared unto him in a flame of fire out of the midst of a bush, he looked and behold the bush burned with fire and the bush was not consumed. And Moses said I will now turn aside and see this great sight, why the bush is not burnt. And when the Lord saw that he turned aside to see, God called unto him out of the midst of the bush, and said Moses, Moses, and he said Here Am I. And he said, Draw not high hither put off thy shoes from off thy feet, For the place where on thou standeth is holy ground.'*

For you to be used by God you must come out of your past, your knowledge and you must be clean and pure. For our God is Holy and He uses the Holy;

> *II Timothy 2:20-21 'But in a great*

*house there are not only vessels of Gold and of silver, but also of wood and of earth, and some to honor and some to dishonor. If a man there purge (cleanses) himself from these, he shall be a vessel unto honor, sanctified, and meet for the Master's use and prepared unto every good work.'*

It's your responsibility to cleanse yourself from the clutter and be available for the use of the master. God is in the business of looking for somebody who he can use and send. There is a lot of work to be done in the kingdom of God but many people - even believers - are busy doing their own things, busy looking for wealth, riches and other worldly things while the Lord is calling the church to Himself

*Matthew 6:33 'But seek ye first the kingdom of God, and His righteousness, and all these things shall be added unto you.'*

We should seek first the kingdom of God and all the things of God; righteousness, faithfulness obedience, humility etc. When we do that all other things physical and spiritual will be added unto us. When you put God first in your life, you will never regret because he will also put you first in his plans and agendas. Make God your partner in business, marriage, ministry and whatever you do and you will never regret. Make him your confidant, your best friend, your closest friend and by doing that your life will be smooth and enjoyable; you won't hustle like others. You will have enough time to work, rest, sleep and you will have enough time to seek him and to worship him. He is looking for the true worshippers who will take their time to go before his presence thanking him and praising him every time not only when they are looking for jobs, spouses, children and new opportunities. God is waiting for you to have a big room for him in your heart. He stands at the door of your heart knocking and asking: "who is ready to receive me that I can make him my instrument of worship and praise." God is looking for faithful stewards who are ready to go for him

*Matthew 9:37-38 'The harvest*

*truly is plenteous, but the laborers are few. Pray ye therefore the Lord of the harvest, that he will send forth laborers into his harvest.'*
There is a lot of work in Gods vineyard.

## *From a Zero to a Hero*

I was very happy when I realized who I am in the kingdom of God.

When I was far from God, without salvation, being disobedient and doing whatever I wanted I was just a zero. You may see yourself a good person; a handsome man or a beautiful woman but as long as you are outside the will of God you are a zero.

Life without Jesus is a zero life; an empty life. It's all in vain to live without Jesus.

*Ecclesiastes 1:1 'all is vanity, vanities of vanities.'*

Life without Jesus has a vacuum which nobody can fill except God. I lived a bad life before I gave my life to Jesus and I didn't know that I needed to ask for the mercies of God.

*II Corinthians 5:17 'Therefore if*

*anyone is in Christ Jesus, he is a new creature, the old things are passed away, behold they are become new.'*

I learnt through experience and decided to give my life to Jesus. When I invited him into my life, things changed and I started a new, sweet life.

In Exodus 3; When God appeared to Moses in the wilderness as a burning bush, he spoke to him of the plans he had upon his life and how he wanted to use him to deliver his children (Israelites) out of slavery in Egypt. Moses felt as if he was a zero; he couldn't go. He told God he couldn't talk to Pharaoh because he was a stammerer. However, God told Moses that He was very ready to use him with his weakness.

This is how I was when God called me to the full time ministry. I argued with him for a long time; I had excuses that everybody can understand and reason.

# 4

# My
# Journey

# My Journey

*"Sometimes it's the journey that teaches you a lot about your destination"*
*Drake.*

I was a foreigner in America; I had just come from Africa to work and get a lot of dollars like other folks. But God said, "I want to use you to preach my gospel all over the world and you will be my witness so prepare yourself." I struggled with God, telling Him that He needed to understand that I am in a foreign land; I couldn't survive without working because I have a family and we needed to pay all the bills. I was trying to make God understand me; I wanted him to fit in my schedule instead of me fitting in his schedule. In 2009 God spoke to me and told me to start a non denominational fellowship in my house. We started and it grew very well and people used to come into our apartment. A few weeks down the line the apartment management asked us to move. They said we were making a lot of noise when singing and praying, and we were using all the visitors packing on that fellowship day. We moved and let a house elsewhere. By the mid 2010, God told me to look for a church building and let with my/our money. I and my husband agreed to obey God and we looked for a building. On 10$^{th}$ October 2010 we officially started a church and all went well. However, in a span of 4 months the building had some infrastructural defects; bathrooms were leaking, everything in that house was in a mess. When the department of Health visited the scene they told us that we needed to move out as soon as possible because the building posed a health hazard to its occupants. So we moved back to the house and many members who had started the church with us left. Only four members and our nuclear family continued having fellowship in our house until January 2011; when we secured another for our church services. God started bringing other new members and we increased in number consistently. At the time I was a part-time pastor, so I worked very hard together with my husband so that we can have enough money to pay our bills and church bills. When we approached some new members, they started paying their tithe faithfully and giving offerings; so we worked as a team and the burden slightly eased. God started showing me the vision he wanted me to carry and I was a bit scared because it seemed so big for an African woman. That is when He told me, "I want you to be a full time pastor and do the work of the Kingdom and I promise to do yours." I refused because I wanted God to understand that in America you cannot survive without working. God continued calling me; sending people to tell me to surrender my life to him and I could not change my mind. I was telling him, "I will serve you and still do my job and get money." It was on March 2012 when God wanted to show me that I can stay without working because I do not own my life. I got very sick and was hospitalized for fourteen days and was discharged to continue with medication at home. After one week I called the company that I worked for and I told them I am ready to go back to work since I was feeling better. They sent me a schedule to go to work. I went for the first and second day and went back home well. On the third day I was too sick to work. I had reported for work but within two hours I asked my supervisor to get somebody to relieve. The following morning I had a severe headache. I asked my husband to take me to the hospital and was hospitalized again for four days. After being treated the doctor told me that I could go home because I was better. I was very happy. I went home and stayed for two weeks; then called my supervisor and asked for schedule. I got a placement and went back to work for one week. My health deteriorated the week that followed. I was taken to hospital in an ambulance and was hospitalized again for four days. While in the hospital, God sent His servant to come and tell me to surrender totally to God or suffer. I told the servant of God I would think about it because I had not decided on the way forward. One night while in the hospital God spoke to me and gave me the schedule he want me to follow on being discharged from hospital. I was very keen. God instructed me saying, "I want you to build an altar where people can come and worship me and start daytime prayers Monday through Friday from 12:30pm – 2:00pm. Whether people will come or not be there in time and offer me worship every day. It wasn't easy to decide but I talked to my husband, Pastor Ephantus and he said he couldn't oppose God or say no to what God had said. He told me to do as the Holy Ghost led and said. So I surrendered all my life, strength, power, time to God since June 2012. July 02$^{nd}$ 2012 is the day we started lunch hour prayers officially and the same day prophet Immanuel Audre was born in my house. He's a son to my daughter. Although life has not been smooth, I have gone through ups and downs and the Lord has been faithful to me, my family and the church.

Our church is called Tabernacle Temple of Praise (TTOP). I was given this name by the Holy Ghost. We preach the holiness of God without compromise and we rely on the leading of the Holy Ghost because he is the promised gift to the latter church.

When Jesus ascended to heaven he told the disciples to go to Jerusalem and wait for the helper to come so that they can be equipped with power to prepare them for the great work that lay ahead. So they stayed in Jerusalem at the upper room till the Holy Ghost descended on them. They were all in one accord and received the gift from God who is the Holy Ghost. We believe in the baptism by immersion; the way Jesus was baptized by John.

I have been facing a lot of opposition in many ways. The devil has been trying to show me how I can't do the work of God in my life; how it's not possible to be in full time service. Since June 2012, I decided to serve God with all my knowledge, power, wisdom and strength regardless of who is for or against my calling. I don't regret being a pastor in life. I don't strain myself to serve him; I just feel I am in my right place of calling and I honor God for choosing me. There are many challenges in ministry, but when you focus on the one who called you, you will make it. During my first days and months in ministry I was not mature enough and when problems came, I could ask God questions upon questions: God did you really call me? If you did am I supposed to suffer lack? And many more but the Grace of God, I am maturing step by step, right now whether I have what I need or not I don't ask question instead I ask for sufficient grace of God to help me overcome.

Would you like to be a Hero of Jesus? In the bible we read about many people whom God called when they were powerless and knew nothing.

Exodus talks about Moses calling. He was not ready to go for God. He tried to excuse himself from the God given assignment. However, God fits in the weaknesses of his own children. When you feel you can't do anything is when God steps in to able you to do his work. God doesn't call the qualified ones; He qualifies the ones He calls. Moses was not a qualified candidate; he had many failures in life; he couldn't talk fluently; he was not very much patient; he was a man of anger. Out of the weaknesses of Moses God found a deliverer of the Israelites. Through Moses God destroyed the land of Egypt and all the belongings.

*Exodus 4: 21-26 'And the Lord said unto Moses, when thou goest to return into Egypt, see that thou to all those wonders before Pharaoh, which I have put in thine hand, but I will harden his heart, that he shall not let the people go .And thou shall say unto Pharaoh, Thus says the Lord, Israel is my son, even my firstborn. And I say unto thee, let my son go, that he may serve me, and if thou refuse to let him go, behold, I will slay thy son even thy firstborn.'*

If you are a bible reader, you can testify and witness with me that Moses was a hero; a mighty man of God; from being a zero man; a stammerer a man of anger God transformed him and used him as a hero. Not only men, God can use women in a mighty way and he has used them before

*In Judges 4: 21 'Then Jael, Heber's wife, took a nail of the tent, and took a hammer in her hand , and went softly unto him, and smote the nail into temples and fastened it unto the ground ,*

*For he was fast asleep and weary so he died.*'
Sisera was an enemy of the army of Israel and God delivered him into the hands of just a simple woman. A house wife; a woman who used to be at home cooking, washing dishes, making beds so she was like a zero woman, not famous, not very much educated, not very much organized like the women of today, but thank God that from a zero person he can get a hero person. Jael was used by God out of many women, civilized, beautiful and smart women. When Jael was in her kitchen or her compound busy doing her normal duties, God just transformed her and made her a strong, brave, courageous woman to kill a mighty man who bothered the armies of the Lord. Out of zero, God can get a Hero. You may be a zero person today; an alcoholic, drug addicted, a prostitute but out of you God can get a great Hero for his own glory. You only need to understand why you were created and the purposes of God concerning your life. Then you will need to release yourself to God the Holy Ghost to just work on you and when he

makes you, you will be a mighty man of valor and a great woman of integrity to his own glory.

# 5

# Men
# of
# Faith

# Men of Faith

## David

In 1<sup>st</sup> Samuel 17 talks about David and Goliath. Goliath was a champion of the camp of philistines and he was against the Israelites and all the armies of God.

*1<sup>st</sup> Samuel 17:1-13, 1:17, 1:20, 1:27, 1:30, 1:34-37, 1:40-41, 1:45-46,1:50, 1:54 'Now the Philistines gathered together their armies to battle, and were gathered together at soco which belongeth to Judah, and pitched between soco and Azekah in Ephesdammim. And Saul and the men of Israel were gathered together, and pitched by the valley of Elah, and set the battle in array against the philistines. And the Philistines stood on a mountain on the other side, and Israel stood on a mountain on the other side, And there was a valley between them. And there went a champion out of the camp of the philistine, named Goliath of Gath, whose height was six cubits and a span. And he had a helmet of brass upon his head* *and he was armed with a coat of mail and the weight of the coat was five thousand shekels of brass. And he had greaves of brass, upon his legs, and a target of brass between his shoulders. And the staff of his spear was like a weavers beam, and his spear's head weighed six hundred shekels of iron and one bearing a shield went before him. And he stood and cried unto the armies of Israel , and said unto them, why are ye come out to set your battle in array am not) a philistine, and ye servants to Saul? Choose ye a man for you and let him come down to me. If he be able to fight with me and to kill me, then we will be your servants, but if I prevail against him, and kill him then shall ye be our servants and serve us. And the Philistine said, I defy the armies of Israel this day, give me a man that we may fight together. When saul and all the Israel heard those words of the philistine, they were dismayed, and greatly afraid. Now*

*David was the son of the Ephrathite of Bethlehem- Judah whose name was Jesse and he had eight sons, and the man was an old man in the days of Saul. And the three eldest sons of Jesse had gone after Saul to the battle. And Jesse said unto David his son, take now for thy brethren an ephan of this parched grain, and these ten loaves, and carry And David spake to the men that by him, saying what shall be done to the man that killeth this philistine, and taketh away the reproach from Israrel? And people answered him after this manner, saying so shall it be done to the man that killeth him. And returned away from him toward another, and spake after the same manner and the people answered him again after the former manner. David said unto Saul, Thy servant was keeping his father's sheep, and where there a lion or a bear and took a lamb out of the flock. I went out after him, and smote him and delivered it out of his mouth,*

and when he arose against me, I
caught him by his beard and smote
hi, and slew him. Thy servant
smote both the lion and the bear,
and this uncircumcised philistine
shall be as one of them seeing he
hath defied the armies of the living
God. And David said, Jehovah who
delivered me out of the paw of the
lion, and out of the paw of the
bear, He will deliver me out of the
hand of this Philistine. And Saul
said unto David, Go, and Jehovah
shall be with thee. And he took his
staff in his hand , and chose him
five smooth stones out of the
brook, and put them in the
shepherd's bag which he had, even
in his wallet , and his sling was in
his hand , and he drew near to the
Philistine. And the philistine came
on and drew unto David, and the
man that bare the shield went
before him. Then said David to the
philistine , thou comest to me with
a sword , and with a spear , and
with a javelin, but I come to thee
in the name of Jehovah of hosts,

*the God of the armies of Israel whom thou has defied. And this day will Jehovah deliver thee into my hands, and I will smite thee, and take thy head from off thee, and I will give the dead bodies of the host of the philistine this day unto the birds of the heavens , and to the beasts of the earth, that all the earth may know that there is a God in Israel. So David prevailed over the Philistine with a sling and a stone, and smote the philistine, a slew him, but there was no sword in the hand of David. And David took the head of the philistine and brought it to Jerusalem, but he put his armor in his tent.'*

I have indicated along passage of the bible concerning David and Goliath, so that we can know how God operates and how he works wonders. David was a Zero; a small boy; shepherd; a man who stayed away from other human beings. He used to live alongside animals in the forest but God turned him from a zero boy to a hero. David trusted in Jehovah and he knew him very well because, when he had some animal attacks in the wilderness, nobody was there, but Jehovah was always with him to fight for him.

When the Lord is on your side, he makes your useless and hopeless life to be useful and hopeful. He turns things around for you. The God of David is an unchangeable God; He's the same yesterday, today and forever. It's only in God in whom our strength is renewed and we have eternal hope. Outside God there is struggle, strife and competition but God protects his own and shows mercy to them that love him. It's only in God that you can be shaped to become a vessel of honor; God will turn your weak point to be your powerful point for his own Glory.

### Zarephath Woman

In 1Kings 17:8 we read about a widow who had only one meal for her and her only son and then die but God knew her more than she did. God sent Elijah to the Zarephath woman so that He (God) can bless her. She didn't have a refrigerator to store food; she had only the last supper (dinner). When Elijah came to this woman, he asked for a glass of water which was not a big deal to the woman because maybe she had many litres of waters. When she was on the way to go and bring water, Elijah added something on top, he said bring me bread also. Now the woman was shocked because she knew what she had in the house was just for her and her son to eat and then die. But this woman got a revelation: 'This man maybe a Godsend. Let me do as he says and she went and made bread and brought it to the servant of God and the prophet spoke these words;

*1Kings 17:13 'Fear not, go do as thou hast said, but make me thererof a little cake first and bring it forth unto me and afterward make for thee and for thy son, For thus says Jehovah the God of Israel. The jar of meal shall not waste, neither shall the cruse of oil fail, until the day that Jehovah sendeth rain upon the earth.'*

This woman benefited through her obedience. She obeyed the word of God through his servant and God fulfilled his promise to the widow; throughout the famine she lacked nothing. This woman was a hero because she gave all what she had to the servant of God without fearing what the boy will eat. She gathered her strength in the Lord and decided to serve God first. Before Elijah had come to the life of this widow, it seems her life was not going well. She was in her Zero point; not knowing what to do or where to go after having the last one meal. That's a hopeless situation; it's a zero situation but God just appeared and through her obedience through her faith, God made her a hero for his glory. Having nothing in your life cannot stop God from blessing you. Some day God will turn things around. Being a zero cannot stop God from making you A Hero. Hallelujah.

There is a woman who was very poor and Jesus observed people when they were giving offerings in the temple and he saw a woman who had two mites and gave all.

*Luke 21:3-4 'And he said, of a truth I say to you, this poor widow*

*cast in more than they all For all
these did of their superfluity cast
in unto the gifts, but she of her
want did cast in all the living that
she had.'*
That means out of her poverty; she gave
God the best. Are you ready to give God
your best? Do you give God leftovers of
everything? Do you give God what you
don't want? We should learn to give God
the best like this woman. This woman
was a hero of faith.

### Abraham

*Genesis 22: 2-3, 9-12 'And he
said, take now thy son, whom thou
lovest even Isaac, and get thee into
the land of Moriah. And offer him
there for a burnt offering upon one
of the mountains which I will tell
thee of . And Abraham rose early
in the morning and saddled his
donkey, and took two of his young
men with him. And they came to the
place which God had told him of.
And Abraham built the Altar there,
and laid the wood in order and
bound Isaac his son, and laid him*

*on the altar, upon the wood. And Abraham stretched forth his hand, and took the knife to slay his son. And the angel of Jehovah called unto him out of heaven and said , Abraham , Abraham And he said , here I am, And he said ,lay not thy hand upon the boy , neither do thou anything unto him. For now I know that thou fearest God, seeing thou hast not withheld thy son, thine only son from me.'*

When Abraham didn't have a son and he was old; he was a hopeless man and was not happy at all until when God gave him a son of promise - Isaac. We can see Abraham was a hero of faith. He had to sacrifice the only son to him because of the love he had with his maker. Are you ready to give God the best out you? Are you ready to be made a hero out of a zero? Heroes come from zeros through the power of the Almighty God.

Many of us believers are so selfish that even to pay their tithe (10% of your increase) is a problem, They don't want to part with it; they struggle to pay to God what belongs to him and yet they are born again Christians, spirit filled, going to heaven but when it comes to be faithful with their increase, they don't want to pay up. Remember Abraham had Isaac only; and was the only son of the promise but when God asked for him, Abraham couldn't question God or struggle with him.

*Malachi 3:8-10 'Will a man rob God? Yet say, wherein have we robbed thee? In tithes and offerings. Ye are cursed with a curse for ye rob me, even this whole nation. Bring ye the whole tithe into the store house that there may be food in my house, and prove me now here with, saith Jehovah of hosts, if I will not open you he windows of heaven, and pour you out a blessing that there shall not be room enough to receive it. '*

God can make you a hero through your giving, if you want to overcome poverty and lack, be a giver. Give to the kingdom of God; give to the needy; give to widows and orphans.

*II Corinthians 9: 6-7 'But this I*

*say, he that soweth sparingly shall reap also sparingly, and he that soweth bountifully shall reap bountifully. Let each man do according as he hath purposed in his heart, not grudgingly, or of necessity for God loveth a cheerful giver.'*

Your giving can promote you from a zero to a hero. The Zarephath woman became a hero through her giving. Before Elijah visited her she was a poor widow and she was waiting to eat her last meal so that she and her only son can die, but when Elijah was connected to her by God, her life changed from that very day.

*I Kings 17:7-16 'And it came to pass after a while, that the brook dried up because there was no rain in the land. And the word of Jehovah came unto him saying, Arise, get there to Zarephath, which belongeth to Sidon, and dwell there, behold, I have commanded a widow there to sustain thee. So he arose and went to Zarephath, and when he came to the gate of the city behold, a* widow was there gathering sticks, and he called to her, and said, Fetch me I pray thee, a little water in a vessel that I may drink. And as she was going to fetch it, he called to her, and said bring me I pray thee, a morsel of bread in thy hand. And she said, As Jehovah liveth, I have not a cake, but a handful of meal in the jar, and a little oil in the cruse, and behold, I am gathering two sticks, that I may go in and dress it for me and my son, that we may eat it, and die. And Elijah said unto her, fear not, go and do as thou hast said, but make me thereof a little cake first, and bring it forth unto me, and afterward make for thee  and for thy son. For thus saith Jehovah, the God of Israel. The jar of meal shall not waste, neither shall the cruse of oil fail, until the day that Jehovah sendeth rain upon the earth. She went and did according to the saying of Elijah, and she and he and her house, did eat many days. The jar of meal wasted not,

*neither did the cruse of oil fail, according to the word of Jehovah which he spake by Elijah.'*
The Zarephath woman was a zero woman; poor, with nothing. Nobody recognized her in the city but when she took a step of faith to obey the voice of the prophet of God who was God's representative that time, she was lifted from a zero to a hero. And that's why we read about this woman even today. Walking in obedience to God can lead you from a zero to a hero. Elijah walked with God hand in hand until he was no more. That means he was taken in a whirlwind to heaven in chariots of fire. Elijah and Enoch are heroes because they never tasted death; they were taken to heaven by God.

*II Kings 2:1-2 'And it came to pass, when Jehovah would take up Elijah by a whirlwind into heaven went with Elisha from Gilgal. And it came to pass, as they still went on. And talked that behold there appeared a chariot of fire, and horses of fire which parted them both asunder, and Elijah went up*

*by a whirlwind into heaven.'*
This passage proves that Elijah did not
die and so he was a hero, he didn't
experience natural death at all.

> Genesis 5: 24 *'And Enoch walked
> with God and he was no more, for
> God took him.'*

The servant of God Enoch also did not
suffer the natural death, he was taken by
God, he was so close to God until God
took him and went with him to heaven.'

## Becoming a Hero for Jesus

It requires you to take a radical decision,
so that God can turn your life from
nobody and make you somebody. You
need to know what God says about you.

> Jeremiah 1:5 *'Before I formed you
> in the belly I knew you, and before
> thou camest forth out of the womb
> I sanctified you, I have appointed
> you a prophet unto the Nation's.'*

Sometimes in life we underrate
ourselves not knowing who we are and
the devil takes advantage of our
ignorance. The devil starts to show us
how useless we are; how we are nothing;
how we can't accomplish anything until

your faith in God is disillusioned. God says that he knew you before you were formed in your mother's womb; He chose you and designed you to be a great man of valor or a great woman of integrity, but the devil and the struggles of life push you far from the will of God or far from the plan and the purpose of God. It's your time to rise up and realize how gifted you are as long as you are alive and God is counting on you, he's calling you to come out of zero life and get into a hero life.

> *Psalms 139:13- 16 'For thou didst form my inward parts Thou didst cover me in my mother's womb. I will give thanks unto thee, for I am fearfully and wonderfully made. Thine eyes did see mine unformed substance, And in thy book they were all written, Even the days that were ordained for me, when as yet there was none of them.'*

You must understand very well who you are now the past notwithstanding. Your past failures cannot stop you from entering into your destined future. Don't allow your past to hinder you from moving forward. It's true you were not able to do what you tried; you failed but don't stop there. God has good plans for your future.

> *Jeremiah 29:11 'For I know the thoughts that I think towards you, saith Jehovah, thoughts of peace and not of evil, to give you hope in your latter end.'*

The devil may bring negative reports in life; your doctor can say what your ears don't want to hear; your senior boss can say something that you were not ready for but remember that the creator of heaven and earth (Jehovah) has good plans for you today and forever. Don't allow the disappointments and the discouragement of the devil hit you like a tornado or a tsunami. Arise, shake the dust and tell the devil, "get *thee behind me Satan For I know who I am and who God says I am; I am not a victim, I am a victor; I am not poor, I am rich; I am not the tail, I am the head; I am not defeated I have conquered; I am not the last, I am the first; I am not beneath, I am above.*"
A hero must know how to fight every opposition and every negative agenda of

the enemy. Nehemiah conquered the opposition. When he came to rebuild the ruined walls of Jerusalem there arose a group who opposed him and ridiculed him too, Sanbalat, Tobias and the others. The bible records a Canaanite woman who went for help from Jesus. She was very much frustrated by the answer that Jesus gave her but she didn't lose heart. She continued persisting until the Lord was touched by her faith and he granted her the desire of her heart.

*Matthew 15:22- 28 'And behold a Canaanite woman came out from those borders, and cried, saying, "Have mercy on me, Oh Lord thou son of David, my daughter is grievously vexed with a demon. But he answered her not a word, And the disciples came and besought him saying send her away for she crieth after us. But he answered and said, I was not sent but unto the lost sheep of the house of Israel. But she came and worshipped him saying, Lord help me. And he answered and said, it is not meant to take the bread of the children and cast it to the dogs. She said, Yea Lord for even the dogs eat of the crumbs which fall from the masters table. Then Jesus answered and said unto her, "Oh woman, great is thy faith, be it done unto thee even as thou wilt." And her daughter was healed from that.'*

If you have persistence, you can be a hero. This Canaanite woman was far away from the blessings of Abraham, Isaac, and Jacob; that means she had no inheritance at all (according to the word of God). She was a "zero"- a Canaanite or a gentile- but her faith pushed her to a level of being a hero and that's why she's being mentioned in the bible.

- You need to believe in yourself. Don't listen to what people say about you, or don't listen to what the devil says about you. You need to start believing in yourself and start confessing positive things and start declaring who you are. *Deuteronomy 28:13 'And Jehovah will make you the head, and not the tail, And thou shalt be above only*

*and thou shall not be beneath.'*
You need to know that you are the greatest architect of your life. You have all the ability to shape yourself and become what you want to be. If you want to be a zero (a nobody) you allow every negative staff in your life; you will accommodate them and wait for the bad results. However, if you want to be a hero (somebody) you can plan and organize yourself not to allow anything negative into your mind. Occupy your minds with positive things and be busy always trying to manage your own life. For you to be a manager of a home or a group, you must be a manager of yourself. Idle mind is the devil's workshop. Don't be an idle minded person; occupy your minds by reading books, bible. Give attention to anything that can strengthen you to become a mighty man in the community; in the Nation; in the church and in the family. I want to challenge men with the love of Christ to take their positions back. They were meant to be the heads of families, communities, churches. God designed men from His creation to be heads and

leaders. Some of the men have stepped out of their God ordained offices. They are no longer there, they don't want responsibilities, and they want to live a simple life without anyone bothering them. God is calling you back to your assigned offices and to your responsibilities. God created Adam first and he gave him the mandate and Authority over all the animals and everything. The woman came after, when God saw that the man should not live alone, he created him a helper who can stand by him, support him through all his work and assignments.

Some men have stepped backward; they have resigned from their duties – the reason why we have a lot of cry in families. Divorce rates are also notably high. May God restore every man and woman to their original assignments so that they can accomplish the purposes of God under the heavens. When you realize the purpose, plan and assignment of God in your life, you will start to yield to him so that he can shape you and mold you for his own purposes.

In the bible we read about many
people who God called; were not
ready and couldn't qualify but thank
God, He doesn't call the qualified
ones, he qualifies the ones He calls.

## Gideon

*In Judges 6:11- 17 'And the Angel
of Jehovah came and sat under the
oak which was in Ophrah, that
pertained unto Joash the
Abiezrite, and his son Gideon was
beating out wheat in the
winepress, to hide it from the
Midianite. And the angel of
Jehovah appeared unto him, and
said unto him, Jehovah is with
thee, thou mighty man of valor.
And Gideon said unto him, Oh my
Lord if Jehovah is with us, why
then is all this befallen? And
where are his wondrous works
which our fathers told us of,
saying Did not Jehovah bring us up
from Egypt? But now Jehovah hath
cast us off, and delivered us into
the hand of Midiah. And Jehovah
looked upon him and said Go in*

*this thy might, and save Israel from the hand of Midiah: have not I sent thee? And he said unto him, Oh Lord wherewith shall I save Israel? Behold, my family is the poorest in Manasseh, and iam the least in my father's house. And Jehovah said unto him, surely I will be with thee and thou shall smite the Midianites as one man. And he said unto him, if now I have found favor in thysight, then show me a sign that is thou that talkest with me.'*

Gideon was amongst those people who were not very ready to do God's assignment because they had suffered a lot in his generation. God had left the Israelites because of their disobedience. When God decided to restore the Israelites, he appeared to Gideon. Gideon had never had an encounter with God; he had heard about God and his wondrous works but he didn't know how God operates. He asked God for a sign to prove that God is the one sending him to fight the Midianites.

Today we have known God and so we

don't need to fear or ask for signs. We need to pray for God to confirm to us by sending other people to confirm or in anyway he may use. When you realize that you have a call of God in your life, you should seek him and start to prepare yourself. Don't delay; don't question God. He has good plans for you and when he calls you he knows you are well able to do his work regardless of your past and failures.

Gideon felt he is not worthy to carry God's assignment because of poverty and being the least in the family. God saw great potential in the life of Gideon and he called him a mighty man of valor. Don't dwell on your past or your failures. Allow God to make you. Gideon was greatly used by God. At the time of going to the battle he went with a group of three hundred men out of thirty-two thousand men. He believed in God and went and fought the Midianites and he won the battle. Today we can call Gideon a hero of God. In the first place Gideon could not believe in himself because of his background and status; they were very poor; he was the least in his family. Once he realized that God saw him and called him a mighty man of valor he gathered strength and believed in God. At times we need to look ourselves in God's eyes (heavenly eyes) not earthly eyes.

## Joseph

He was the son of Jacob through Rachel, and Jacob loved him greatly. He was a dreamer. Whenever he dreamt, he shared with his brothers and parents. His brothers hated him for his dreams; and also because he was loved by the father. One time his father sent him to check on his brothers who were taking care of their father's flock in the wilderness. When they saw him coming from a far, they plotted to kill him so that he won't go back to the hands of the father who loved him.

> *Genesis 37:3 'Now Israel loved Joseph more than all his children, because he was the son of his old age, and he made him a coat of many colors*
> *4. And his brethren saw that their father loved him more than all his*

brethren, and they hated him, and could not speak peaceably unto him

5. Joseph dreamt a dream, and he told it to his brethren and they hated him yet and more.

9. And he dreamed yet another dream,and told it to his brethren and said behold, I have dreamed yet a dream,

12. And his brethren went to feed their father's flock in Shechem.

13. And Israel (Jacob) said unto Joseph, Are not thy brethren feeding the flock in Shechem? Come, and I will send thee unto them And he said here am i.

18. And they saw him a far off, and before he came near unto them, they conspired against him to slay him.

19. And they said one to another, behold this dreamer cometh.

20. Come now therefore, let us slay him and cast him into one of the pits, and we will say, And evil beast hath devoured him, and we shall see what will become of his

dreams.

21. Reuben heard it, and delivered him out of their hand, and said let us not take his life.

22. Reuben said unto them , shed no blood, cast him into this pit that is in the wilderness, but lay no hand upon him that he might deliver him out of their hand, to restore him to his father.

23. And it came to pass , when Joseph was come unto his brethren, that they stripped Joseph off his coat , and the coat of many colors that was on him.

24. And they took him, and cast him into the pit, and the pit was empty, there was no water in it.

25. And they sat down to eat bread and they lifted up their eyes and looked, and behold, a caravan of Ishmaelites was coming from Gilead, with their camels bearing spicery and balm and myrrh, going to carry it down to Egypt.

27. Come and let us sell him to the Ishmaelites, and let not our hand be upon him, for he is our brother

our flesh. And his brethren hearkened unto him.

28.And there passed by Midianites merchant men, and they drew and lifted up Joseph out of the pit,and sold Joseph to the Ishmaelites for twenty pieces of silver. And they brought Joseph into Egypt.

31. And they took Joseph's coat and killed a he- goat and dipped the coat in the blood.

32. And they sent the coat of many colors and they brought it to their father and said, this have we found, know now whether it is thy son's coat or not.

33. And he knew it, and said, it is my son's coat, an evil beast hath devoured him, joseph is without doubt torn in pieces.

34. And Jacob rent his garments, and put sackcloth upon his loins and mourned for his son many days.

36. And the Midianites sold him into Egypt unto Portiphar, an officer of Pharaoh's the captain of the guard.

This is a long passage about Joseph and it shows us how he was loved by his own father and how he was hated by his own brothers. Joseph was a polite cool guy, a God fearing and humble. He was a down to earth man, but his brothers hated him for the dreams and for his progress. Do you know that anyone who has a dream or a vision is a hero in some way? And that person has many enemies; Joseph was hated and sold to Egypt by his own brothers. They were born of the same father but different mothers, and they couldn't spare him though he was of their own bloodline. A visionary is a hero and must be very strong to fight every opposition. For you to be a hero, you must have come from somewhere. You don't sleep some day to wake up a Hero some other day. A visionary has many enemies who are ready to pull him down so that his vision or dream can be aborted.

# 6

# A Hero
# is
# a Fighter

# A hero is a fighter

*"A hero is someone who has given his or her life to something bigger than oneself."*
Joseph Campbell

When we come a little bit in the worldly things like politics, we see some people who have fought for their countries, communities, families etc
In Kenya, for instance, we had the first President of the Republic of Kenya. The late Mzee Jomo Kenyatta led the fight Kenya's independence and freedom. Many other Kenyans lost their lives; were detained, imprisoned and suffered a lot on behalf of Kenyan people. Mzee Kenyatta was a Hero - he fought for his country and his people.
We have another African man - The late Nelson Mandela of South Africa. Many of us know about his story; how he sacrificed for his own people and country to have freedom. He was imprisoned for many years; he spent almost all his life in prison but thank God when he was released he became the first Black African president in South

Africa. Mandela was a hero - he fought for his country and his people.

- For you to be a hero in the kingdom of God- You must release yourself to God. You must surrender totally to the Lord's calling and be ready to take all the assignments he gives you.

*John 10:10 'Jesus came that we may have life and have it abundantly*

*11. I am the good shepherd, The Shepherd layeth down his life for the sheep.'*

Jesus Christ our Lord and savior gave himself for us the (world) so that he can restore and reconcile mankind with God again. He gave himself as a sacrifice and he suffered for the world to get saved. Jesus has set a good example and he's greatest mentor. We need to follow him and do according to his word and obey all his instructions. The apostles obeyed the Lord and followed him with all their hearts and they accomplished the will of God in their time.

Men; God is calling you to be the heads of your families and also be representatives of the Lord's kingdom.

Be men of honor; love your own wives and families. Demonstrate the love of God to your family and after you have done that, you can go out there with the blessings of your family because your house is in order. Every ministry you do will be successful because your family is backing you. When somebody starts to preach the kingdom, your own home (family) is your Jerusalem. You will then extend the gospel to Judea, Samaria and all the corners of the earth. Many people are very good in preaching Judea, Samaria and other places. They cannot preach to their own families because they don't portrait Jesus in the homes. They are very good out there, but if you can ask their spouse and children about his behavior, they will say what they know about him. Most of the time, the opinions are contrary to what other people know about him. Start to evangelize in your own homes. Let everybody and everything in your family know that you are "A Man of God." Let them testify of your salvation and when you pass that test, it will be very easy to do God's work and to reach many in other places.

Likewise, women be submissive to your own husbands and be respectful to them. Let your children know that you have the honor of the man of the house (HUSBAND). You are a WIFE and a MOTHER in your family, regardless of your status in your work place. Let them see a difference in you. Let your husband and children testify of your humility and goodness as a wife and mother- Be a virtuous women and a hero *Proverbs 31:10 'A worthy (virtuous) woman who can find? For her price is far above rubies*

*11. The heart of her husband trusteth in her, And he shall have no lack of gain*

*12. She doeth him good and not evil All the days of her life*

*13. She seeketh wool and flax, And worketh willingly with her hands.*

*14. She is like the merchant ships, she bringeth her bread from a far.*

*15. She riseth also while it is yet night and giveth food to her household, And their task to her maidens.*

*16. She consideth a field,andbuyeth it , with the fruit of her hands, she planteth a vineyard*

*17. She girdeth her loins with strength, Andmaketh strong her arms*

*18. She perceiveth that her merchandise is profitable; her lamp goeth not out by night.*

*19. She layeth her hands to the distaff, and her hands hold the spindle*

*20. She stretcheth out her hand to the poor yea, she reacheth forth her hands to the needy*

*21. She is not afraid of the snow for her household, for all her household are clothed with scarlet*

*22. She maketh for herself carpets of tapestry, her clothing is fine linen and purple*

*23. Her husband is known in the gates, when he sitteth among the elders of the land*

*24. She maketh linen garments and selleth them, and delivereth girdles unto the merchants*

*25. Strength and dignity are her clothing, And she laugheth at the time to come*

*26. She openeth her mouth with wisdom And the Law of kindness is on her*

*tongue.*
*27. She looketh well to the ways of her household. And eateth not the bread of idleness*
*28. Her children rise up and call her blessed. Her husband also, and he praiseth her, saying*
*29. Many daughters have done worthily, but thou excelled them all.*
*30. Grace is deceitful, and beauty is vain, but a woman that feareth Jehovah, she shall be praised*
*31. Give her of the fruit of her hands, And let her works praise her in the gates.'*

A virtuous woman is a woman of integrity; she's a hero by herself. Her work and character is known by the family and neighbors. She sets a good example on how a woman who fears God lives. The bible talks about her and her husband. To those who have no earthly husbands, you have Jesus as your sweetheart and everlasting love who can never leave you nor forsake you. He's the best husband; even the married women rely on Jesus as their first husband. You are the one to demonstrate the love of Jesus to your family and your neighbors. Let your children know that you are "A Woman of God." Let them testify like the children of the virtuous woman in the book of proverbs.

Women have a big role in their families and everywhere than anybody else. Women are life givers, hope givers, restorers, healers, counselors, advisers, administrators and leaders. Women have a big heart and are not quick to quit. They stand firm even when things are not okay. They can afford a smile in the midst of chaos. They can say its ok when things are falling apart. Many women, especially God fearing women are Heroes. When God created a woman, He was very careful to make a wonderful creation. God was so much organized when making this wonderful being called a woman.

Women are wonderful creation who they know how to adapt every situation. A woman grows up in her parents' home. When she becomes an adult, she gets married and moves out of her parents and she goes and join another family she know not and starts referring to them as her own; my husband, my father, mother, brother, sister in-law and she stays there forever. That's how this wonderful creation was made by the creator. Bless the Lord for women. They make their families look wonderful; they decorate their houses; they help their spouses and their family members; they make the decision to leave their parents and relatives to go to another home.

For marriages and homes to succeed and be strong, both the man and the woman need to leave their own families and be joined together to start their own family. If they live on the husband's family properties or houses, the husband should be full of wisdom so that he can be able to love his wife without interference from anyone. Sometimes men are controlled by their fathers and mothers and do not have enough time with his own wife. He can't make his own decision until the parents interfere. This sometimes turns to be dangerous to the marriage.

Marriage is between two - a man and a woman only. That doesn't mean that you will not respect his parents and the family, or her parents and the family. *Genesis 2:24 'Therefore, shall a man leave his father and his mother, and shall cleave unto his wife, and they shall be one flesh.'*

*Matthew19: 5 'And said, for this cause shall a man leave his father and mother, and shall cleave to his wife, and the two shall become one flesh*

*6. So that they are no more two but one flesh. What therefore, God hath joined together, let no man put asunder.'*

Some parents contribute to the separation or divorce of their children. Parents should be careful because the bible says what therefore God hath joined together, let no man (you included) put asunder. Parents should be wise when it comes to dealing with your grown up kids who are married. Parents should love their daughter in – law and accept her because she is the choice of your son, not your choice. Parents should respect and accept your son in-law the way he is because he is the choice of your own daughter and she left many men and chose that one. We should respect the decisions our children or parents make. Let's support them to reduce the rate of divorces and separation in our communities; even in churches and homes.

When Paul was talking to Titus about elderly mothers, he had this to say

*Titus 2: 1 'Speak thou the things which benefit the sound doctrine*

*2. Aged men be temperate, grave, sober minded, sound in faith, in love, in patience*

*3. That aged woman likewise, be reverent in demeanor, not slanders nor enslaved to much wine, teachers of that which is good,*

*4. That they may train the young women to love their husbands, to love their children*

*5. To be sober- minded, chaste, workers at home, kind being in subjection to their own husbands, that the word of God be not blasphemed.'*

The work of mothers is to train their daughters how to love their own husbands and children; and how to behave well in their marriages and families; love them, advice them. Be far from them so that they can build their own homes. Set a good example to your sons and daughters and they will always admire you and respect you. A wise woman who knows how to build her house can be a hero not a zero.

*Proverbs 14: 1 'Every wise woman buildeth her house, but the foolish plucketh it down with her own hands.'*

We should be wise and build instead of being foolish and destroy our houses. Your house can be many things; your family, your life, your work, your career, your community, your church etc. Are you wise in all these areas of life? Are you a builder or a destroyer of your house or church? Many people have the 'anointing' of destroying everything that is good instead of building and supporting that one which is good. In the bible we see a woman who destroyed her own family

*1$^{st}$ Kings 21: 4 'And Ahab came into his house heavy and displeased because of the word which Naboth the Jezreelite had spoken to him, for he had said, I will not give thee the inheritance of my fathers. And he laid him down upon his*

*bed, and turned away his face, and would eat no bread.*

*5. But Jezebel his wife came to him, and said unto him, why is thy spirit so sad, thou eatest no bread?*

*6. And he said unto her, Because I spake unto Naboth the Jezreelite, and said unto him, give me thy vineyard and for money or else, if it please thee, I will give thee another vineyard for it, and he answered, I will not give thee my vineyard.*

*7 And Jezebel his wife said unto him, dost thou now govern the kingdom of Israel? Arise, and eat bread, and let thy heart be merry. I will give thee the vineyard of Naboth the Jezreelite.'*

Jezebel was an evil woman and she made Naboth to be killed, she made an evil plan using name of the King Ahab her husband in secret until Naboth was killed. It's evil to shed innocent blood because of the things of this world that are perishable. Jezebel grabbed the Naboth's vineyard but if you continue reading the bible, you can hear what befell on her.

Be wise and build the kingdom of God,

your family, your community and all other areas that the Holy Ghost will lead you.

### *Learn from Myself*

By the grace of God, I can write to encourage you who have been called and feel like quitting the ministry; you feel that now you are at the end of your life. I want to take this moment to let you know that if it's God who has called you, you will make it no matter what comes your way. The toughest thing in life is if you called yourself or people called you. When you think you can do something by yourself this is when you will fall in a big pit. Those God has called will be able to accomplish the purposes and the plans of God irrespective of the storms and obstacles. When God called me to work for him here in the United States of America, I was not ready at all. Circumstances couldn't allow me to be one of his trusted and faithful servants in the U.S.A. I had many excuses just like Moses or Gideon; education wise I couldn't; financial status I couldn't. I felt disturbed; not the person that God had been looking for.

However, God appeared to me many times and he confirmed to me that he's calling me to full time ministry through some servants of God - some of whom I knew them; some of whom I didn't. I used to tell God that I am a foreigner and couldn't be a voice of God in America – a place for powerful, well known, established men and women of God. You can't escape God. You can escape a gun, an accident, a Tsunami an earthquake or any other kind of danger but you can't escape the hand of God. There are some people who tried to run away from God in the bible, they had many excuses like me and you; Moses, Gideon, Jonah, and others who felt they can't do the work of God for many problems they were going through. Moses said to God that he didn't know how to talk well; Gideon said he was the least and the poorest in the 12 tribes of Israel; Jonah was not ready to see the people of Nineveh saved and healed by God. He changed his mind and instead of going to Nineveh where God had sent him, he went to Tarshish where he caused a big loss to the businessmen of tarshish because he changed his direction from Nineveh address to Tarshish., He tried to hide under the ship so that no one can know what was going on, but God followed him.

You can't hide from God; when you put your bed down in hell, he will still follow you. God followed Jonah even when he went underneath. The hand of God is long enough to get you from your hiding place; his eye is too sharp to see you in that dark hideout. Answer to His call; surrender to him and you will have rest and peace.

To be honest, I was one of the people who said, 'This is not my time to serve God,' considering that I received prophecy earlier on that God will take me to a far country where I will go and serve him. I felt strange being in a foreign land; not very much educated; not very much smart; I didn't have money; my accent; my color. I found myself telling God, 'let me serve you in the church as an ordinary member just as other people.' I want to tell you that God doesn't call the qualified ones;

those who are well able - he qualifies those he has called and makes them His own vessels so that they can live for Him and Him alone.

*Psalms 113:7- 8 'God lifts the poor and the needy from dust and ashes heap That He may seat Him with princes, with the princes of his people.'*

This is what God can do and that's what he has done to me - this Kenyan woman. I was far from the promises of God; I was not ready to receive all his offers because of fear and intimidation. That has changed. Now I'm a changed person; a strong woman to fight for God's kingdom and that's why I can say like Paul

> *Romans 1:16 'For I'm not ashamed of the gospel of Christ, for it is the power to salvation for everyone who believes.'*

Now I'm not ashamed; I fear nothing because I know He who called me is faithful and just. I'm ready to serve my God with all my strength, knowledge, understanding and wisdom. I have decided to follow him and to obey all his instructions as a fulltime minister. It has not been easy since I accepted to be in full time calling. I have been through many issues.

Being a pastor of a small group and with many obligations; paying the church building rent, bills, undertaking various programs is not easy. Sometimes, I experience a deficit in finances but God has been faithful to us. I thank God for the little flock he has given me to shepherd. They are serious people; committed to the work of God and carry the vision with us. May God continually bless this precious family of Tabernacle Temple of Praise (TTOP) in the Holy name of Jesus Christ) our Lord and savior. May they be expanded spiritually, financially, materially and physically so that they can continue with the work of the kingdom of God. We are blessed with wonderful people who pay their tithes faithfully – the reason why we are able to preach the gospel in U.S.A.

We also have other ministries outside the U.S.A. We support some girls in Kenya (Rift Valley Province). We supply sanitary pads to two hundred and forty-two girls for the glory of God.

We also lift Jesus high with our money through the radio preaching in one of the radio station in Seattle - Salem communications. We are on air every Sunday night at 8pm to 8:30pm pacific time;

*John 12:32 'If I am lifted up above the earth, I will draw all men to myself.'*

When we got that revelation we decided to lift him with our money through the radio and it has been going well. People call us for prayers and words of encouragement when they listen to our radio preaching. We also have new members joining the church after they listen to us from the radio.

If you would like to be blessed together with us, log on to KGNW.com at the scheduled time and location:

Pacific Time – 8:00pm-8:30pm
Mountain Time-9:00pm-9:30pm
Central Time 10:00pm-10:30pm
Eastern Time – 11:00pm-11:30pm
The name of our programme is the HOUR OF THE LORD'S VISITATION from

Tabernacle Temple of Praise, Federal way, WA. May God bless you when you tune your radio or you go to the internet. I'm writing all this information to show you that God doesn't work in numbers; He's able when you are few; he's able when you are many. He's the commander of the great Army; He owns cattle on a thousand hills; Silver and gold belongs to him. Your number is not important. What matters is the measure of your faith for God to move in your midst. Elijah was alone when he prayed a prayer to God and said, 'let there be no rain on earth for three and a half years.' God honored the prayers of his prophet.

*James 5:17 'Elijah was just as human as we are, and for three and a half years his prayers kept the rain from falling*
*18. But when he did pray for rain it fell from the skies and made the crops grow.'*

I have learnt to trust God even when things seem not to work. I have seen the faithfulness of God. If you know that the Lord God has called you for his work, don't hesitate to answer his call. Don't wait until he sends people; prophet after prophet; don't wait until he touches you. Take a step of faith and make a radical decision and say yes to him and make some declarations. Then, you will see how good and sweet it is to serve God. Its only in God that I have this confidence; That I'm called to serve a great God and a conqueror no matter what; I'm a Hero of God; and I know he is taking me from glory to glory.

Before I came to the U.S.A, I used to do some business in Kenya-Africa. I never rested; I never had joy and peace. I experienced all kinds of worries of life. I had a calculator, a pen and a book beside my bed. In the middle of the night I could get up and start doing some calculations which didn't add up. Sometimes I felt good and had peace in my business, but most of my life was full of worries and anxieties; not knowing the outcome of my business. However, now I praise God I'm very happy to serve this wonderful kingdom; that I just wait to be instructed by the Holy Ghost. Every day I rely on him totally; I listen very carefully to what He tells me and pay attention to all instructions. Thank God for it's from glory to glory. Sometimes I contested the instruction having in mind the congregation God has entrusted me. According to me, it's not easy. Today, however, if he tells me to plan for a million-dollar project, I can agree it because I know how he operates. He has enabled me to grow and to mature and to understand that He owns everything as the Bible says

> Psalms 24:1 'The earth is the Lord's and all its fullness, The world and who dwell there in.'

When you know that you don't survive because you are a rich person, or you are married or you have sons and daughters or you are a doctor etc, that's when you will have peace and rest. We don't stand with our strength anymore but by the strength of the Lord.

> Psalms 20:7 'Some trust in chariots, and some in horses, but we will remember the name of the Lord our God.'
>
> Psalms 121;2 'My help comes from the Lord, who made heaven and the earth

*3. He will not allow your foot to be moved, He who keeps you will not slumber.*

*4. Behold He who keeps Israel(you) shall neither slumber nor sleep*

*5. The Lord is your keeper; The Lord is your shade at your right hand.*

*6. The sun shall not strike you by day, Nor the moon by night.*

*7. The Lord shall preserve you from all evil, He shall preserve your soul*

*8. The Lord shall preserve your going out and your coming in from this time forth, and even forever more.'*

These passages make us understand that neither money, nor family, nor priorities is the answer but Jesus is.

You can buy a house but its God who gives you sleep. You can be a Hero of God regardless of your money and riches. When you trust in God and allow God to lead you; you will win all your battles and live a successful life. Money cannot give you a successful life without

God being involved. Nothing can work well for you in God's absence. Involve God in your life, family career and all that.

> *Proverbs 3:5 'Trust in the Lord with all your heart, And lean not on your own understanding,*
> *6. In all ways acknowledge Him, And he shall direct your paths.'*
> *Psalms 125: 1 'Those who trust in the Lord Are like mount Zion which cannot be moved, but abides forever.'*

Trusting in God will make you firm and strong; nothing can move. Trusting men can fail you. Trusting your knowledge can fail you but when your trust is in God you will never fail.

> *Jeremiah 17:5 'Cursed is the man who trusts in man and makes flesh his strength, whose heart departs from the Lord.'*


## Get Down to Work

You can't make it without God. Your effort cannot make you. Don't mistake me: I don't mean you shouldn't work, think and exploit your potential. The underlying foundation is to trust in Jehovah the maker of Heaven on Earth; then you do your level best, because God hates lazy people – laziness is not allowed in the bible

> *II Thessalonians 3:10 'For even when we were with you, we commanded you this, if anyone will not work, neither shall he eat.*
>
> *11 For we hear that there are some who walk among you in a disorderly manner, not working at all, but are busy bodies.'*

If you are called by God to be a full time minister, there must be an assignment for you to accomplish. He makes sure you get all provision because you are an employee of the kingdom of God. When you faithfully execute your assignment; and you become patient; in due time you will enjoy in the Lord's vineyard. God never call people to do nothing. God never called people who did nothing. In the bible we have witnessed those people that God called from their works to his.

• Moses was a shepherd. He took care of his father-in-laws sheep when God appeared to him. God called him to be a deliverer of the children of Israel. He was called to be sent; not sit down.

- Abraham was called by God from his own family, household to go to a far country to be a father of many nations. When God calls you, you must rise up and go somewhere. You must leave your own priorities and engage yourself to God's priorities.
- Elisha was called from his farming business to follow Elijah. He soon received the mantle after Elijah's departure. When God is calling somebody there must be a key task to be accomplished in his kingdom.
- The disciples were called from different offices to follow Jesus. Some were fishers and Jesus told them to follow Him so that they can be fishers of men.

When God calls you, make sure that you authenticate your call; make sure you know the purpose for your calling; make sure you locate your position and be established. In our life today people are fighting in the work of God because many don't understand their positions. They want to do what others are doing and also what they are comfortable with. Everybody today wants to be a pastor, a prophet, an apostle, an evangelist or a teacher without seeking to know God's purpose and position for you. In all these callings many are fighting to position themselves "strategically" the will of the Father notwithstanding.

Saul who became Paul was called from persecuting the church to be a great apostle whom God used greatly to save the gentiles and also Jews. There are some in our midst who serve God because they don't have anything to do. For you to come and serve God, you must come from somewhere. God uses His power to convince you to stop what you are doing and come and serve him. I have heard many servants of God saying how God dealt with them until they surrendered all to God. Some leave big businesses while others quit lucrative jobs. Many of those who answer to the call are often misunderstood from almost all perspectives; (family, marriage, friends, community, colleagues, etc.) When God called me to full time ministry I used to work as a nurse assistant. I worked many hours from different agents. In a pay check of two weeks, I would have earned 1,500 dollars or more; I would make above 3,000 dollars every month. I had come from Africa with big dreams; upgrading my family, building big houses; buying land in Kenya; becoming a great, rich woman. In those big dreams the voice consistently reminded me, "This is the place I said many years that I will bring you so that you can serve me." I pretended not to hear, and continued working from job to job, company to company. One time I gathered strength to argue with God; I wanted him to understand me and fit in my agendas. I started by telling God, "I'm a foreigner in this land, and for me to live in a foreign land I have to work hard so that I can be able to pay all my bills; send some of my money to Kenya for some projects; help my family members who are not well able. Let me work part time and be your servant, whenever you need me, I will be available." God said to me, "I need you to be full time in my work. The harvest is plenty but we don't have enough laborers." Inside my heart I was saying, "Why don't you call those who are stable, established and citizen of America? Why call a poor woman who has millions of burden to accomplish with her month to month salary?" This did not stop God from calling me to full time ministry until when He came and proved to me that I don't survive because of working many hours; or because of the money I earn; or because I'm married; or because I have kids and grandkids; or because I have family here in America and in Kenya.

He allowed the enemy to touch my body and I was in and out of hospital from March 2012 till June 2012. While in the hospital for the first time God sent a prophet who told me what God had told him and I promised to think about it. For the second time I was so sick that another servant was sent to come and anoint my feet; and to declare that I'm going to full time ministry. He obeyed

and did all what God has said. While in
the hospital for the third time many
people came to see me and to pray for
me. I had booked for ticket to Texas to
attend a conference by one International
preacher from Kenya: Reverend
Teresiah Wairimu Kinyanjui of Faith
Evangelistic Ministries in Kenya and
Britain (FEM) and Teresiah Wairimu
Evangelistic Ministries in U.S.A
(TWEM).
In Kenya, I was one of the followers of
mom Teresiah. Closer to the conference
dates, I tried to convince the doctors to
discharge me (so that I could attend the
conference in Texas). I didn't tell them
I wanted to travel but that was my idea.
The doctors gathered in my hospital
room and discussed my condition for a
half an hour. One of them told me,
"Elizabeth, you can't go home because
you must remain on the life support
machine for some few days." So I called
one of my sisters in Christ whom we
were to go with; wrote a note to the
woman of God asking her to pray for me.
When they went, I continued to trust
upon God for my healing. I remember

one evening I reminded the devil that I was going to see my savior, my lover and He is still with me here. I told the devil he's are a liar and a looser.

When the conference was going on, one night God spoke to the woman of God concerning me and the following day she called an altar call according to what my sister, Bernice Gichwiri, told me. She ministered through the word of knowledge and said, "In our midst there's somebody who was sent by a servant of God who is very sick in Hospital bed, can you come here?" Sister Bernice delayed a little bit until the servant of God pointed on her and she called her in the altar. When she went there, I was prayed for and she was given a word to tell me. The stewards during the conference were told by mum Teresiah to call me after prayers and ask me whether I experienced the power of God. They were told to give me this word

> Psalms 118:17 "I shall not die, but live. And declare the works of the Lord."

The prayer took place at 11:00am local time and definitely I felt the power of

God that moment. It hit me like an electric shock through my body. I felt extraordinary power. At that time we were with two other servants of God who had come to see me and I witnessed to them. A few minutes later I received a call from Sister Bernice and other intercessors. They told me what mum had said; the prayers she prayed for me and I received my total healing in Jesus name.

Since that day my whole body was healed and the swollen neck was healed completely to this day. The doctors could not believe that I was healed; but they witnessed the change in my body. The doctors had sent in a hospital chaplain to prepare me for eventual death. Some nurses used to come to my bed advising me how it's good to write a will before I die.

Deep inside I knew I was not dying before preaching the gospel to Pakistan and other countries in the world. When I was very young spiritually, God told me that I will go to preach to Pakistan and that's why I said no to death, I could see it coming and many people were waiting for me to die even our Kenyan people. Some had started to plan how to take the remains of Elizabeth back to Kenya. On the contrary, I stood by faith not knowing how God will come, but nevertheless, He came and healed me. Do you know why I was healed? God wanted me to be a Testimony; a witness of his healing power and mercies that endures forever and ever. Amen.

You could be having a testimony of healing like me or even a powerful than mine. I want to let you know that you were delivered from the hands of death so that you can work for God. The devil meant it for evil but God meant it for good; that's why I'm alive to work in his vineyard. I have given one of my testimonies so that you can know that when God is in need of you, you can't run from him. After all the struggle and pain, I answered to the call of God and we agreed with my husband and the family that we will put God first in everything. It hasn't been easy but by God's grace we are pressing on. Dear brethren, don't quit; continue pressing on. There is a reward and it's so sweet to serve knowing that you are called. If you are not a full time minister, do your work and support the ministry; or the church; or the work of God according to the leading of the Holy Ghost. For the believers who are not full time workers in God's vineyard there are also giftings. Some are called to be supporters, intercessors, ushers, deacons, deaconess, givers, etc. You need to locate your position so that you can execute the mandate and get your blessings.

Serving God is an honor and a privilege. Do not take it lightly. Don't think that people give their money to church because they don't have needs; they give because they love God. For the love to be complete there must be a giving.

> John 3:16 "For God so loved the world that He gave His only begotten son...."

A husband gives himself to the wife; in the same way, a wife gives herself to the husband. In every form of relationship there must be giving. We exchange gifts with the friends and people we love. Giving to a certain department (in church, family, community, etc) proves your commitment and sacrifice. This shows that you value whatever you are giving towards. If you love your church, pay your tithes faithfully; give your offerings; plant seeds; give yourself too for prayers and avail yourself. This is a sign of surrender for your finances, time and strength and you will be richly blessed.

I have seen God open doors in my life when I give. One time I was going through a tough financial wilderness in Kenya (over ten years ago). We were going to church with my family and in my pocket I had 100 Kenya Shilling (equivalent to one dollar). I had planned to give 50 shillings for offering and 50 shillings to buy food for my family. The man of God who was preaching said, "It's time to trust God in our giving and give God what you have in your pocket even if it was for food, trust God and give the whole amount." I saw the Holy Ghost pointing at me saying, "Elizabeth did you hear that?" "Yes Lord I did, but I don't have food for my family" I responded. The voice came back to me,

"Give all money, your watch and your handbag. (I had a new handbag valued Kenya Shillings 1,500 - equivalent to $15). The case became a little bit complicated. I felt faith inside me; I took a plastic bag and put all my stuff in. I took the watch, the purse and the Kenya Shillings 100 to the altar of God with a lot of tears.

On handing over my sacrificial offering to the man of God, He looked at me and prophesied, "You are blessed and God will use you in a mighty way to support mission work; you will go to a far country where you will serve God full time." When I heard that word, I laughed at myself saying, "Poor Elizabeth, you have nothing." But I said, "God let your will be done." After the church service my family asked me to go to buy food before heading home. I told them, "We won't go to the store first because the sun is too hot for us. Let's go home first. We will go to the store later in the evening." Then, I didn't want to tell them what happened in the church. I felt conviction that the Lord will visit me in His own miraculous ways; that my family will not sleep without food. It was at 2:00pm Kenyan time when we walked back home about 1.5 miles to our house. On reaching home, there was nothing to cook or eat. I went direct to my bedroom and knelt down beside my bed and I started to thank God for His faithfulness.

Two hours later, somebody knocked our door. She came in and said, "I have brought you this envelope and I don't want to stay for I'm going somewhere else." She gave me the envelope and left. I went to my bedroom, opened the envelope and found Kenya Shillings 10,000 ($100 dollar equivalent). I thanked God unreservedly. The following morning, I got up and went to the pastor in his office holding Kenya Shillings 1,000 for tithe and I gave him the testimony. We bought food and met many needs with that miracle money. I just wanted to share that to everybody who is in a tough corner; without food for the family, I want you to know that our God is able to supply everything you need.

*Philippians 4:19 'And my God*

*shall supply all your needs according to his riches in glory by Christ Jesus.'*
I have many testimonies about God and my financial life in Africa and also in America. It has not been easy to be a minister in a foreign land where God calls you to full time ministry. You have your family and bills to be paid, rent and other financial needs everyone has. Jehovah Jireh has been my God. He has been my present help in time of need and has promised not to leave me nor forsake me.

*Deuteronomy 31:8 'And the Lord, He is the one who goes before you. He will be with you; He will not leave you nor forsake you, do not fear nor be dismayed.'*
Whenever God promises not to leave you nor forsake you, you have the assurance that all is well. Whatever comes your way, you will be able to stand firm and conquer every battle from within and without. Bless the name of the Lord. He is Jehovah Saboath – The Lord who fights our battles. He fought for King Jehoshaphat and the Israelites.

*II Chronicles 20: 17 'You will not
need to fight in this battle position
yourselves, stand still and see the
salvation of the Lord, who is with
you O Judah and Jerusalem. Do
not fear or be dismayed.'*
When God says that he will fight your
battles, you should believe him and let
him fight all your battles.

## Taking Charge

You must have faith in God; you must
believe what the word of God says about
your life. The book of Psalms shows us
that we were designed by God to be like
him. It will take the faith you have in
God and the powerful hand of God to
come out of the level of a zero. You must
have a positive attitude towards your
life and yourself. Don't believe in the
enemy's report; believe in the report of
the Lord. He created you uniquely.

*Psalms 139:13 'For you formed my
inward parts, you covered me in
my mother's womb
14 I will praise you, for I am
fearfully and wonderfully made,
Marvelous are your works. And*

*that my soul knows very well.'*
*Genesis 1:27 'So God created man*
*in His own image, in the image of*
*God He created him, male and*
*female He created them.'*
When you realize that God created you
in his own image and likeness, you start
to behave as a person of dignity. You are
fashioned the way you are by God. God
created a man to be a hero but the devil
popped in and tried to make a man a
zero. In the Garden of Eden, Adam was
the senior boss; the CEO; the Managing
Director; The Chairman; The President.
When the devil arrived and started to
communicate with eve his wife,
everything went wrong. He dropped from
a Hero to a Zero; the glory of God
departed from them when they ate the
forbidden fruit. God had given Adam
instructions in the beginning what to do
and what not to do; what to eat and what
not to eat.
However, the thief just appeared to
steal, kill and destroy all the plans of
God in the Garden of Eden.
For you to be a hero you must listen,
obey and follow all the instructions from

God without missing any mark. Adam and Eve disobeyed God; they listened to the enemy and they fell from God's Glory.

When somebody gets born again, he takes the salvation of God as a holy garment and he clothes with the glory of God at all times. When somebody backslides and sins before God, this garment is taken away and he's left naked. That's why Adam realized that they were naked when they committed sin before God. The glory of God had departed from them and they could not withstand God's presence when he visited them in the garden. A hero must be ready to listen to God, follow all instructions and be sensitive in the spirit. You must have the spirit of discernment. You must know who you are in God; not in the world.

The devil tries to make you a zero but God's plan and purpose is to make you a hero of faith like Daniel, Shadrack, Meshack, Abednego, Joshua, Gideon, David, Joshua, Paul, Peter and many others. Even women, God made Deborah, Abigail, Esther, Mary, Jael, Sarah,

Elizabeth and many others to be His mighty heroes.

Esther was an orphan; she was raised by her uncle Mordecai. She was a zero with nothing but God shaped her from a zero to a hero. She was chosen to be the queen in a foreign land in the midst of many women; she won favor before King Xerxes.

Your background doesn't matter; you need to rise up and believe that Jesus came to lift those who are downcast; to give status to those who have none; to heal the broken hearted. Through Jesus the zeros will rise to be heroes, thank God. Allow Jesus to mold and shape you.

### *Giving can make you a hero*

> *1Kings 17: 10-16 'So he arose and went to Zarephath; And when he came to the gates of the city, indeed a widow was there gathering sticks. And he called to her and said, please bring me a little water in a cup that I may drink.*
>
> *11 And as she was going to get it, he called to her and said, please*

*bring me a morsel of bread in your hand.*

*12 So she said, "As the Lord your God lives, I do not have bread, only a handful of flour in a bin, and a little oil in a jar, and see I am gathering a couple of sticks that I may go in and prepare it for myself and my son , that we may eat it and die."*

*13 And Elijah said to her, do not fear, go and do as you have said, but make me a small cake from it first, and bring it to me and afterward make some for yourself and your son*

*14 For thus says the Lord God of Israel, The bin of flour shall not be used up, nor shall the jar of oil run dry, until the day the Lord sends rain on the earth.'*

The woman, full of faith and obedience; not asking a single question, went and made the first piece of bread to the prophet. She was blessed beyond measure - from a poor widow (a zero) to a rich woman (A hero). Giving towards Gods work can promote you and make

you a great man/ woman in your city.
Give God the best and put Him first in
your life and you will witness his
goodness and faithfulness. This woman
was a woman of faith; she obeyed and
followed the prophet's instructions and
orders. Sometimes we miss the mark
because we don't want to apply the faith
in us.
We are very fearful of what will happen
to us tomorrow. This woman believed in
the words of prophet and considered God
first in her life. That's how Christians
or believers ought to be. Let's trust in
God so that we can be established; and
also trust in the prophets for us to
prosper (II Chronicles 20:20).
God is calling you to come out of fear,
intimidation, reproach etc and become
one of His mighty man / woman. Be a
Hero of God; fight for God; stand for
God; go for God. Be what God intended
you to be from the beginning of creation.
God chose you before you were created
in your mother's womb.

*Jeremiah 1: 5 "Before I formed
you in the womb I knew you, before
you were born I sanctified you, I*

*ordained you a prophet (Hero) to the nations."*

*6 Then said I "Ah Lord God! Behold I cannot speak for I am a youth."*

*7 But the Lord said to me, 'Do not say I am a youth,' For you shall go to all whom I send you, And whatever I command you, you shall speak.*

*8 Do not be afraid of their faces, For I am with you to deliver you "says the Lord.*

*9 Then the Lord put faith his hand and touched my mouth and the Lord said to me "Behold, I have put my words in your mouth*

*10 See I have this day set you over the nations and over the kingdoms, To root out and to pull down, To destroy and to throw down, To build and to plant.*

Don't allow the devil, people or circumstances to interrupt with what was designed by God many years ago. You are called to be a Hero; a Winner; and a Conqueror. Don't listen to the lies of the devil.

*John 10:10 'The devil comes to kill, to steal and to destroy, but Jesus came that we may have life and have it more abundantly.'* Jesus came to make us his own heroes; fighters; warriors. You are a hero as long as you believe in Jesus and you have faith in him. Allow him to build you up and strengthen you so that you can become what he has designed you to be. The word of God is the light to our paths; the food of life; the water that cleanses us; the water that quenches our thirst; the sword to cut everything that is ungodly; the hammer to break and destroy every evil structure in us; the key to every kind of a blessing and to every promise that the father has for us; our daily medication to every kind of sickness and disease; the source of hope, joy and peace.

# 8

# The Word
# Can Make You
# A Hero

# The Word Can Make You a Hero

*"We must allow the Word of God to confront us, to disturb our security, to undermine our complacency and to overthrow our patterns of thought and behavior."*
John R.W. Stott

It's by the mercies and goodness of God that we are forgiven and changed. We were not a people before but now are:

> *1Peter 2:9 'But you are a chosen generation, a royal priesthood, a holy nation, His own special people, that you may proclaim the praises of him who called you out of darkness into his marvelous light.*
> *10 You once were not a people but now are now a people of God, who had not obtained mercy but now have obtained mercy.'*

We were not a chosen generation and we were not God's special people until Jesus came into our lives transformed us, and made us righteous by the washing of his holy blood. Now you are a new creation, you are blessed, not cursed, if you are in Christ Jesus.

Nobody and nothing can take you away
from God. Nothing is able to separate
you from the love of God.

> *Romans 8:35 'Who shall separate*
> *us from the love of Christ? Shall*
> *tribulation or distress or*
> *persecution or famine or*
> *nakedness or perish or sword?*
> *37 Yet in all these things we are*
> *more than conquerors through him*
> *who loved us.*
> *38 For I am persuaded that neither*
> *death nor life no angels nor*
> *principalities nor powers, nor*
> *things present nor things to come*
> *39 nor height, nor depth, nor any*
> *other created thing, shall be able*
> *to separate us from the love of God*
> *which is in Christ Jesus our Lord.'*

Friends, nothing and nobody will
separate us from the love of Christ or
God. You are called in such a time as
this to do something for the kingdom of
God. You are the vessel that God is
waiting for do what he has called you to.
There are many responsibilities in the
kingdom of God; you don't need to be a
pastor or bishop to serve God. You can

serve God at any level and to your capacity. You can serve as an intercessor, usher, giver, volunteer in the church, support the work of God, help in the church, city or community. Avail yourself; God will show up and give you an assignment. God is looking for somebody to go for him. When you allow God to work on your life, to cleanse you as Isaiah did, then God can find a man or woman out of you to send.

*Isaiah 6:5 'So I said, woe unto me for I am undone! Because I am a man of unclean lips, And dwell in the midst of a people of unclean lips, for my eyes have seen the king, The Lord of host*

*6 Then one of the Seraphim flew to me having in his hand a live coal which he had taken with tongs from the altar*

*7 And he touched my mouth with it, and said Behold this has touched your lips, your iniquity is taken away and your sin purged*

*8 Also I heard the voice of the Lord, saying "Whom shall I send, and who will go for us?"*

*Then I said, "here I am send me".*

Isaiah had to undergo a process of cleansing for him to qualify to be send of the Lord. You can't just come from nowhere and say that you are ready to go for God. You must be cleansed, made righteous to be used in every good work in the kingdom of God.

*1ˢᵗ Peter 1:16 'Be holy because I am holy.'*

God uses holy vessels that have surrendered to him and have decided to follow him in all their lives. God is holy and he uses or works with holy people or vessels. Are you ready to be holy and to walk upright before God so that you can go for Him? When Mary Magdalene was cleansed of the demons, she served Jesus; she sacrificed to buy the most expensive perfume for the Lord before his death.

> *John 12:3 'Then Mary took a proud of very costly oil of spikenard, annointed the feet of Jesus, and wiped his feet with her hair; And the house was filled with the fragrance of the oil.'*

When Mary was delivered from the powers of hell, she decided to serve Jesus with all her strength and power. Mary was a zero who became a hero later; that's why she is recorded in the bible. Serving God and devoting yourself to the work of God can promote you from a zero to a hero. God is in business of shaping and making the zeros to be heroes. God is not a respecter of persons and he's not unjust. He is the rewarder of those who seek him diligently. When you get connected with God, He starts to deal with your zero capacity and attitude. He starts to upgrade you; preparing you to go to the Hero class.

*Psalms 75:6 'Promotion doesn't come from east or west but from God'*

When you walk with God like Abraham did, you will never be ashamed. There is a time Abraham's life was full of zero. He and his wife had grown old; they didn't have a child. He felt a zero kind of attitude and started looking for alternatives. During this time his wife advised him to take their house girl

(Haggai) as a second wife - which was
never in the plans of their maker
(Jehovah).
Some situations in life try to make you
a zero; feeling that there is no hope and
nothing good can come out of what you
are or have. But it's time to encourage
yourself and others in the family, your
church, workmates, and community to
strengthen yourself in the Lord. God is
waiting for you to come out of your
family situation because He has good
plans for you all the time. You have a
better future, don't you worry. You have
a bright destiny ahead of you if you
continue trusting in God.
Train yourself to trust in God all the
time and rely on him totally and you will
never regret. Those who trust in God
shall never be put to shame and they
shall never be shaken.

### Mephibosheth
There is a man in the bible called
Mephibosheth, son of Jonathan (Saul's
son). He was in a zero condition; he
called himself a dead dog. One time
King David remembered the vow he had

made with Jonathan when they were young. He called some officers in his palace asking of Saul's family to show them favor.

*II Samuel 9:1 Now David said "Is there still anyone who is left of the house of Saul, that I can show him kindness (favor) for Jonathan's sake."*

*3b And Ziba said to the king, There is still a son of Jonathan who is lame in his feet.*

*4 So the king said to him, where is he?" And ziba said to the king, "Indeed he is in the house of Machir the son of Ammiel in Lo Debar*

*6 Now when Mephibosheth the son of Jonathan the son of Saul, had come to David, he fell on his face and prostrated himself. Then David said "Mephibosheth?" And he answered, "Here is your servant"*

*7 So David said to him, Do not fear, for I will surely show you kindness for Jonathan your father's sake, and will restore to*

*you all the land of Saul your
grandfather, and you shall eat
bread at my table continually.
8 Then he bowed himself and said,
"What is your servant that you
should look upon such a dead dog
as I?"*

Friends, what God can do; No man can
do. With God all things are possible and
there is nothing too hard for our God.
Praise his holy name somebody!!
God can change your miserable life in a
span of a moment. Mephibosheth was
lame in his feet but that situation did not
stop God from doing a new thing in him.
God gave him favor; it's God who caused
David to remember the vows he had
made with Jonathan. God did all this to
favor Mephibosheth. Mephibosheth
came out of LoDebar to the palace. This
is what God can do; what He has been
doing to his own children. When you put
God first in your life, and surrender
yourself to him, He starts to work
wonders in your life and change your
zero status into the Hero status.
Mephibosheth came out of a zero status
to a hero status; eating from the table of

the King; having a luxurious life in palace after suffering almost the whole of his life. Earlier on He was dependent on others to carry him, feed him, cloth him and do everything for him, but when he entered the gates of palace his life changed completely.

If you want your life to change completely start your life with King Jesus; he welcomes you in his kingdom (palace) where you will never suffer lack or shame again. He will take care of everything that you need.

# 9

# My
# Ministry
# In
# USA

## My Ministry In USA

*"Let every man abide in the calling wherein he is called and his work will be as sacred as the work of the ministry. It is not what a man does that determines whether his work is sacred or secular, it is why he does it."*
— *A.W. Tozer, The Pursuit of God*

I came to the United States of America in June 15th, 2006 and I have been doing many kinds of jobs until I realized why God brought me to America.

Many years earlier, when I was in Kenya, God used many prophets to prophecy to me about my future. They spoke many things I never dreamt of.

One of the major prophecies I got was that "God is taking me to a far country, where he will make me his servant; where I will do his work." That was not in my mind or plans. The Bible is explicit

> *1st Corinthians 2:9 'But as it is written: Eye has not seen, nor ear heard, nor have entered into the heart of man the things which God has prepared for those who love him.'*

I kept on listening to the prophets, one after another, from different places. I kept the words in my heart until January 2006 when I started praying for the United States of America and I started claiming this Nation. I fell in love with her. Every time I heard or saw any material about USA I would listen very carefully and with a lot of concern. I started feeling a connection to USA. Then, I was going through difficult times that nobody understood. No one was ready to help me until when God intervened.

I called the God, who sees, came in and saw all my troubles and problems I was going through:

> Genesis 16:13 "I have now seen the one who sees me. God saw my afflictions and spoke to me and strengthened me."

We started the fellowship in our apartment and it grew very well and very quick. People showed up every Tuesday evening from 7:30pm for a two-hour session. God told me he wanted it to be a non-denominational fellowship. So I invited all churches and many people came. In 1 ½ years, the fellowship had grown to more than forty people until the apartment management started complaining that we are making a lot of noise and we are occupying many parking lots during the fellowship day. So they called notice of vacating from their apartments. After two weeks God graciously blessed us with a house to rent and spoke to me and told me, "I want you to open a church because some of the people who came to the fellowship had no church of their own." It wasn't easy but the Holy Ghost convicted us; I and my husband Ephantus and said yes to God.

We looked for a church facility and got one. We planned on how to open a church and on November 10$^{th}$, 2010 we opened our church Tabernacle Temple of Praise (TTOP) officially. Many people joined us while some came that day to support us.

After three months the building started developing problems. We were told to vacate the building as soon as possible because of health concerns. We went back to the house where almost all

members went away. Only I, my
husband, two daughters, a son and two
church members remained. We continued
fellowshipping in our house on Sunday
and Tuesday.
Two months later, the Lord spoke to me
and he told me, "Elizabeth I want you to
start looking for a church building." We
were so few that inside my heart I asked,
"Who will pay the rent? Where shall we
get the money? The Lord answered, "You
and your husband will do that until you
get more people who will come to
support you." I said to God "if that's the
case who am I to say no? You have to
convince my husband because I don't
want us to fight or quarrel, if it's you
Lord create an atmosphere, where we can
discuss this issue together." The Lord
heard and answered my request. My
husband was very ready to obey the
Lord. I started going round and round
looking for a building that we could
afford.
One morning the Lord directed me to a
vacant building. I booked an
appointment with the property
management for negotiations. I met them

the following day and gained favor. I secured the premise in a week's time. My family and the two members started going to church and within a short time people of African descent started to attend; from Africa, other states and some from our city, including those who didn't have a church to attend. By the grace of God, we have seen the hand of God in our lives. I and my husband catered for the church rent and bills for six months until when people who joined us decided to pop in and carry the burdens together with us. We are now celebrating 6 years of God's faithfulness.

# 10

# About Tabernacle Temple of Praise (TTOP)

## About Tabernacle Temple of Praise (TTOP)

Each day in our church, has been a day of increase and greatness. The few people that the Lord has joined us with are wonderful and blessed. Through their support, we have done some missions and projects in Kenya, Israel and Haiti. We have been able to preach through one of American Powerful Radio stations every week. We have been able to send our First Lady, President and founder (Pastor Elizabeth) to Israel for a biblical tour and many to the glory of God. God has used our church in many ways to support our own Kenyan community. He has moved in a mighty way.

We are not many in our church, but we have been there to support the vision of TTOP. We have no room for doubts on what God says concerning us. The members have been strong and supportive. Since March 2012 I have been a full time pastor; I don't work anywhere else except in the Kingdom of God. It has been a challenge but I made a decision when I realized the plans of

God were concerning my life in
America. I have been in and out of
problems, financial challenges, and
others but my God has been so faithful.
Ministry in the USA has not been easy.
If you don't confirm who called you,
you can quit in the middle of the
ministry. For me, I have been growing
stronger by the day; with or without
money.

I and my family decided to follow all
God's instructions and orders, and I
thank my husband who has been there for
me since God called me as a full time
pastor. My kids, especially the youngest
who is eleven now (2015) have been
encouraging me and telling me that she
loves it when I'm a full time pastor.
Although she doesn't have everything
other children can have she always tells
me, "mama, continue serving God; he
will surprise us one time; he will come
and bless us more than those who are
working in other fields." I have seen
God in my life. God has been so gracious
to me and my family and also to the
church family. TTOP family is the Best.
Hallelujah to Jesus the King of kings.

Being chosen by God is an honor and a privilege and I humble myself. I decrease that the king of glory (JESUS CHRIST) may increase in my life that whatever I do in my life will bring Him glory.

*1ˢᵗ Peter 2:9 But you are a chosen people, a royal priesthood, a holy nation, God's special possession that you may declare the praises of Him who called you.*

After you allow God to shape you and mould you, you come out of a zero person and you become what He says you are. God has chosen you, no matter what people or demons says about you. God has made you a holy Nation by cleansing you with his begotten son's precious blood. You are God's special person. You are not an ordinary man or woman; you are God's own possession - you are God's property. He has done all those things in your life so that you can proclaim the praises of the Lord. The reason why you didn't die last year, last month, last week or yesterday is because God wants you to become his precious vessel who will declare the goodness of the Lord.

> *Psalms118:17 "I SHALL NOT DIE, BUTLIVE, AND DECLARE THE WORKS OF THE LORD."*

The devil has been trying to finish you, in many ways but remind him Psalms 118:17 and silence him in Jesus name. The devil has no power over your life. He tries to pretend to be a lion but he's not; pretends to be the angel of the light but he is not. He was defeated long ago by Jesus Christ on the cross. Praise his name. He is the rock of ages; the chief cornerstone; the Messiah; the Prince of peace; the wonderful counselor, savior of the world.

When I came to realize who my Lord is I felt good and my life changed completely. I don't rely on the mercies of men anymore. To do the work of God in USA where people have the best churches, instruments, vehicles and a lot of money is very intimidating. But the Holy Ghost revealed to me that what I have and carry and whom I serve will pave way for me because it's not about physical or tangible things; it's about spiritual things.

I have come to learn through the
revelation of the Holy Ghost, that USA
needs to know and have The Holy Ghost;
who was promised many years ago by the
Lord Jesus Christ when he said to the
disciples, "go and tarry in Jerusalem and
stay in the upper room for the Helper to
come upon you when I depart from you."
So it was Jesus to ascend and the Holy
Ghost to descend and that's what
happened.

> Acts 2:1 'And when the day of
> Pentecost was now come, they were
> all together in one place
> 2 Suddenly there came from heaven
> a sound as of the rushing mighty
> wind, and it filled all the house
> where they were sitting
> 3 And there appeared unto them
> tongues parting asunder, like as of
> fire, and it sat upon each one of
> them.
> 4 And they were all filled with the
> Holy Spirit and began to speak
> with other tongues, as the spirit
> gave the utterance.'

The church in America is missing
something very important - the power of

the Holy Ghost. When we don't allow the Holy Spirit to move in our churches, being the promised gift from God the father and the son, then we miss the way to go. Jesus said to his disciples, "I will not leave you as orphans" in John 14:18. Jesus would not want to leave the church without a helper or a comforter and that's why we need to invite him (the Holy Ghost) in our lives, marriages, families, ministries and everywhere.

The Holy Spirit is the one who teaches us how to obey and trust God. He reveals who we ought to be in the kingdom of God and everywhere.

When we don't allow the Holy Spirit to rule, reign and lead us, we become religious and we start looking for our own things to please God. It is very hard to please God without the Holy Ghost and faith. USA also needs uncompromised gospel, whether all people will leave you on the pulpit alone; preach the true and full gospel of Jesus Christ.

Don't dilute the word so that you can accommodate many or have many members. It is good to have them but where will you take them if they are not ready for the Kingdom of God (Holiness and Righteousness of God)? Do you have your own place to take all these people you preach to; messing up with the Holy word of God; trying to remove the strict verses in the bible and the serious verses that talks about God's Holiness? *Psalms 99:3 THE LORD OUR GOD IS HOLY*

> *Hebrews 12:14 "Make every effort to live in peace with all men and to pursue holy, without holiness no one (man) shall see the Lord."*

It's good to be a pastor, a leader, a member of a church or congregation but the bible insists very much that "......WITHOUT HOLINESS NO MAN SHALL SEE THE LORD." That means holiness is the key to the things of God. You must be holy and pure for you to be used by the Lord.

Many churches in the world today are not preaching the holiness of God any more. They are preaching that Gospel that pleases people and members so that they can continue to come to church; bring their tithes; ready to do great projects. But remember, every service you do must line up with God's will and the will of God for us is that we all be holy and walk upright before him so that you can inherit the kingdom.

For your work in the Lord to be complete, you must be a registered member in the kingdom of heaven and you will be registered when you receive Jesus Christ as Lord and Savior. You allow his precious blood to cleanse and sanctify you to become pure and holy. Your name appears in the book of life and then you will have a good account in heaven where anything you do will be recorded. That's why God visited Cornelius because he was a giver; he was not a believer and God sent Peter to him. You can be a giver and the principles of giving will work for you and you will be blessed but beyond your giving and your alms, God is calling you for eternal life and the forgiveness of your sin. Giving to God and to his work or giving to people can't qualify you to be Holy. You need to believe in your heart unto righteousness, and with your mouth you confess that Jesus is Lord and then you

receive salvation (Romans 10:10)
*Romans 10:17 'You must hear the word of God, so that you can believe.'*
In Acts 10 God decided to reward Cornelius with eternal life, because he was a good man, a giver and man who feared God. That's why the Holy Spirit sent Peter to Caesarea to the house of Cornelius to go and preach the good news of the kingdom of God. Cornelius and his household believed God, in other words they received salvation (the forgiveness of their sins).

Leaders of churches, let's preach the Christ who died and resurrected from the dead; let's preach the whole truth of the word of God; let's call sin just that - not bad manners so that we can lead people to true repentance. Please don't call people to just be members of your church. Invite them to be members of the kingdom of heaven. Tell them the true word that will pierce their hearts and lead them to repentance.

Preach the truth, speak the truth, live the truth, do the truth, walk the truth of the word of God. Don't call people for church membership only but call them for Heavenly membership. Teach them how they need to live a holy life. Let's not misinterpret the grace of God. It wasn't released for us to continue sinning but for us to stop sinning. The grace came to teach us how to abide in holiness and in the fear of God. The grace of God came to introduce us into new life in Christ Jesus. Let's not misinterpret the grace of God and let's not misuse it.

*Romans 6:1 "What shall we say? Shall we go on sinning so that the grace may increase?"*

Paul asked this question to the people of God; do we need to continue sinning? No, we should be disciplined and we should have the fear of God in us. You should stop sinning and hate sin and be holy as our God who called us. The church continues to sin because the Grace is given but this is not the will of God. You need to control yourself from sinning all the time. Allow the Holy Spirit to lead you and to be the master over your life and you will never fail.

*Galatians 5:16-26 'Walk in the*

*spirit and you shall not fulfil the lust of flesh, those people who practice such things will not inherit the kingdom of God.'*
Your work should follow your holy life, which means, you love Jesus and have accepted him as Lord and Savior and then you accept his promised gift of the Holy Ghost and then you will be good to go. The grace enables us to get closer to God, follow all His instructions and the orders of God but not the contrary. You can't continue sinning if you have a seed of God in you and also if you are a seed of God.

*II Corinthians 5:17 'Wherefore if any man is in Christ, he is a new creature, the old things are passed away, behold they are becoming new.'*
If you have an encounter with the Lord Jesus, your life must change; you start to live a new life. When Saul (Paul) had an encounter with the Lord, his life changed and he was made a great apostle and a big preacher to the gentiles. There must be a change when you receive Jesus Christ in your life as Lord and Savior.

You must bear fruits according to repentance; you must make the name of the Lord known like the Samaritan woman. Before she met Jesus at the well she was a zero; a woman of many husbands; nobody could trust or love her until when he met a man (Jesus) who is above all other men of the world. She thought, "This is a man who can be another husband to pay some bills." Little did she know that he was not an ordinary man. He was the Christ who quenches every form of thirst in your life. It was unlawful for a Jew and a Samaritan to share something together. They were not friends; they were enemies by law. At this point in time the mediator comes in between and does a great job in the life of the Samaritan woman. She was made whole and she started to evangelize. she went to her village and started to talk about a great man who has revealed all her secrets and she spread the gospel in her city.

It's until you have an encounter with the savior of the world that you will be made a hero of his kingdom. You will be used in a mighty way for his glory. Allow the

Lord to shape you and mould you so that you can become a hero -vessel of honor- to be used for every good work. Life without Jesus is as zero as nothing, a branch which is not attached to a tree cannot bear fruits; instead it dries up.

> *John 15: 1 'I am the true vine, and my Father is the husband man (Vinedresser)"*
>
> *2 Every branch in me that beareth not fruits, he taketh it away and every branch thatbeareth fruit, he cleanseth it, that it may bear more fruits.'*

Jesus is the vine, the Father (God) is the vinedresser and we are (church) the branches. For the tree to be complete it must have branches. For Jesus to work in this world he will use us; the tree feeds the branches and the work of those fed branches is to bear more and more fruits. The branch that does not bear fruits is supposed to be cut off to allow the one that beareth to bear more and more. It's God's (vinedresser's) work to cut off unfruitful branch. His work is to go round the tree to see which branch should be removed and which to remain.

Be keen to make sure you bear fruits for
the kingdom of God, be a hero in bearing
fruits, and don't be a zero. God can
change a zero to a hero.

> Ephesians 5:1 'Be ye therefore
> imitators of God, as beloved
> children,
> 2 And walk in love, even as Christ
> also loved you, and gave himself
> up for us, an offering and a
> sacrifice to God for an odor of a
> sweet smell.'

If you want to become a hero in the
kingdom of God you must imitate your
Master (Jesus Christ) as beloved
children. You must also walk in love.
You become a Hero after overcoming all
bad character, behavior, pretense and
you yield to your Master's programmes
and schedules; that means you start to
stay or live a life worth it, like Paul. It
took the hand of God to change Saul's
life and made him a great apostle and
Paul surrendered to the calling of God
and it reached a point he declared some
powerful words in the bible.

> Philippians 1:21 'For me to live is
> Christ and to die is gain.'

Paul reached to a point where he felt that He doesn't exist again but Christ did. When he was called and transformed he decided to live for God and God alone; that means whatever he did, he did it for God's glory. He knew very well that he lived just for Christ and his kingdom; he was ready in and out of season to preach the gospel of grace to the gentiles and all other people, including the Jews. He had zeal to serve God was ready to pay any cost for Christ sake. In Romans he witnessed this:

> Romans 1:14 'I am debtor both to Greeks and to Barbarians, both to the wise and to the foolish.
>
> 15 So, as much as in me is, I am ready to preach the gospel to you also that are in Rome
>
> 16 For I am not ashamed of the gospel; for it is the power of God unto salvation to everyone that believeth; to the Jew first, and to the Greek.'

Before he was called and delivered, he persecuted the church of Christ; he was a zero in the presence of God. He had nothing good before God or in the presence of God; at that time his name was Saul.

> Acts 8:3 'But Saul kept trying to destroy the church, going into one house after another, he began dragging off men and women and throwing them in prison.
>
> Acts 9:3 As he neared Damascus (Saul) on his journey, suddenly a light from heaven flashed around him.
>
> 4 He fell to the ground and heard a voice say to him, "Saul, Saul, why do you persecute me?"

5 Who are you, Lord?" Saul asked
I am Jesus, who you are persecuting, he replied

> 6 Now get up and go into the city and you will be told what you must do."
>
> 7 These travelling with Saul stood there speechless; they heard the sound but did not see anyone
>
> 8 Saul got up from the ground, but when he opened his eyes he could see nothing. So they led him by the hand into Damascus.
>
> 9 For three days he was blind, and

*did not eat or drink anything*
*10 In Damascus there was a*
*disciple named Ananias. The Lord*
*called to him in a Vision,*
*"Ananias" "Yes Lord, "he*
*answered*
*11 The Lord told him, "Go to the*
*house of Judas on Straight Street*
*and ask for a man from Tarsus*
*named Saul, for he is praying.*
*12 In a vision he has seen a man*
*named Ananias come and place his*
*hands on him to restore his sight.'*

The Lord Jesus Christ had to deal with Saul completely to transform him to be an apostle. Heroes come from somewhere. The Lord has to take you through a process until you qualify to be a Hero of Jesus Christ.

Moses had to be taken to the wilderness of Arabia from palace. David had to go through wilderness experience while taking his father Jesse's flock. Joseph had to undergo rejection from his own brother to be sold to Egypt; then taken to prison before becoming a great hero in Egypt.

Pure gold must go through the process of

refining. The more the gold is put into fire, the more valuable and precious it becomes. From A Zero to A Hero, there is a journey and a process to undergo. You can't come from nowhere and call yourself a Hero. A Hero comes from somewhere; from a far off location; and proceeds slowly by slowly, step by step and from glory to glory.

## Jabez

*I Chronicles 4:9 'Now Jabez was more honorable than his brothers, and his mother called his name Jabez saying, because I bore him in pain.*

*10 And Jabez prayed or called on the God of Israel saying, OH that you would bless me indeed, and enlarge my territory that your hand would be with me, and that you would keep me from evil, that I may not cause pain. So God granted him what he requested.'*

Jabez refused to dwell on the negative side of his life; there was a bad record behind his name (pain). He didn't force on that; he knew that God would give him another chance to change his name and life. Jabez believed in himself; he had self confidence. He knew he was not what people or devil said; he knew God's plans and thoughts. He fought and enquired from the Lord. He placed a prayer request before God; which was granted. Jabez was so much blessed and he became a Hero of God. He refused to dwell on the past and he saw himself in his future.

Don't dwell on your past, failures, defeat, shame. Come out and call upon God, and your life will change like that one of Jabez,

> Isaiah 43:18 'Don't remember the former things, Nor consider the things of old
> 19 Behold I will do a new thing, Now it shall spring forth, shall you not know it? I will even make a road in the wilderness and rivers in the desert.'

A zero person is like a wilderness or a desert; but when this person connects with God he becomes a changed person. That's why the bible says that God will make a way in the wilderness; in that hopeless person. God starts to do a new thing in that desert that was dry with no hope; rivers starts to flow, ideas and strategies starts to emerge and he starts to bring forth fruits, hope, expectations and every positive thing and value. This person ends up being a Hero of God. Your past cannot stop you from being who God intends you to be. Just rise up and call yourself a conqueror, change

your behavior, character, come out of
your past failures and don't confess
negative again - don't allow any demon
or anything negative to call you useless.
You are peculiar person. You are a royal
priest hood, a holy nation; chosen of the
Lord Hallelujah!!!!

NOTES

# NOTES

# NOTES

# NOTES